CW00519852

UNDERSTANDIN
PUBLISHERS' CONTF

Michael Legat has spent some fifty years in the book business. During his long career as Editorial Director, first of Corgi Books and then of Cassell, he was also responsible for the wording of the publishing agreements used by those houses. Since becoming a full-time author in 1978, he has published five novels and seventeen non-fiction books. The latter include *An Author's Guide to Publishing, Writing for Pleasure and Profit, The Nuts and Bolts of Writing, Plotting the Novel* and *Revision: An Author's Guide*, all published by Robert Hale. Michael Legat lives in Horsted Keynes, West Sussex.

Understanding Publishers' Contracts

Michael Legat

ROBERT HALE · LONDON

© *Michael Legat 1992 & 2002*
First published in Great Britain 1992
This paperback edition with revisions 2002

ISBN 0 7090 7289 9

Robert Hale Limited
Clerkenwell House
Clerkenwell Green
London EC1R 0HT

Printed by Gutenberg Press Limited, Malta

Contents

This book is dedicated to

Ronald Whiting
(because he is my oldest friend in publishing)
and to
Fred Nolan
(because I am his, I think, and I owe him one)
but also to
Brian Cleeve
(because he started me on my writing career)
and to
Eleanor Corey, Nan Maynard, Diane Pearson, John
McLaughlin, John Hale, John Foster White, Ernest Hecht
and Mark Le Fanu
(because they are all special friends in the book business)
and finally, of course, to
Rosetta
(because she is my dear one)

Foreword

I should like to thank a number of individuals and organizations who have helped me to produce this book. My grateful thanks go to:

John Hale, my publisher, for his confidence in my ability to write the book, and for his helpful comments on the typescript;

John McLaughlin, my agent, for his friendly encouragement, and especially for his detailed and constructive criticisms of the book which have not only provided me with invaluable information, but have saved me from making a number of gaffes;

Kate Pool of The Society of Authors for her helpful information regarding the problems most often raised in respect of their contracts by the authors she deals with;

The Society of Authors and the Writers' Guild of Great Britain for permission to reprint a typical Minimum Terms Agreement;

The Publishers Association for permission to reprint their Code of Practice;

The Association of Authors' Agents for permission to reprint their Code of Practice;

Numerous publishers who were kind enough to send me copies of their printed agreement forms.

*

I should like to make it clear that the views expressed in this book are not necessarily those of my publisher, nor of my agent, nor, indeed, of anyone else. They are mine. I think they are sensible. You must make your own judgment of them.

Then I want to apologise to anyone who is offended by the fact that I have used 'he' and 'him' and 'himself' throughout. I have done so simply because to write 'he or she', 'him or her', 'himself or herself' is clumsy. I find it offensive – not in the sexist sense, but stylistically. Unfortunately, the English language has no satisfactory single word to cover both sexes (one can't really use 'one', if you see what I mean, and 'it' would be even more unacceptable). So, I'm sorry. Please read in the alternative whenever you feel it right to do so, or simply try to think of 'he' being used, as in the past, to cover both sexes in what amounted to an impersonal way, and without any sexist or male chauvinist intentions.

Finally, I should like to warn any publishers who may read this book that their hackles will almost certainly rise as they do so. In its pages I often suggest that you are far from author-friendly, and you will constantly find me encouraging authors to fight for terms which you may consider outrageously generous. But you already have your own guide in that excellent publication, *Publishing Agreements, A Book of Precedents*, edited by Charles Clark, which, while magisterial in its coverage and comparatively liberal in its attitudes, is still somewhat weighted on your side. In any case, you are big boys, and I reckon you can take care of yourselves. Just remember, though, what happened to Goliath, and think what a force he and David would have been if they had been truly on the same side.

M.L.

NOTE TO REVISED EDITION

Although ten years have passed since the first appearance of this book, by far the larger part of the information it contains is still entirely valid and will, I believe, continue to be so. However a number of changes have been made in order to update the text, and especially to add some advice on contracts for electronic rights (see pp. 178–179).

My thanks for help in preparing this new edition go to my publisher, to the late Roger Palmer, to my agent, John McLaughlin, and to Kate Pool of the Society of Authors.

M.L.

1 The Purpose of This Book

As recently as a hundred years ago, at the end of the nineteenth century, the agreements between publishers and authors which covered the arrangements for the publication of a book were usually short and simple – often consisting, indeed, of no more than a brief handwritten letter. In an age when life was less complex, when communications were slower and limited in scope, when universal education was no more than a dream, when publishing was 'an occupation for gentlemen', the short, simple letter was adequate; it could, after all, always be supplemented by another letter, if some new circumstance should arise. And although its simplicity, while apparently allowing easy understanding of its content, may have been lamentably imprecise, authors were rarely likely to argue over the terms, since few of them had agents or other sources of independent advice readily available. Besides, those who ran publishing houses were gentlemen who liked books, and who, because they were well-bred, could be relied upon to behave honourably and to regard a handshake as binding – at least, that was supposed to be the idea, though there were undoubtedly some appalling rogues among them.

During the twentieth century life has become much more difficult and uncertain in many ways; the scope of a literary property has been enormously enlarged – mass markets, bookclubs, films, radio and television, to name just a few major developments, have become commonplace – and world-wide communications take place at the speed of sound (or even of light); the proportion of those leaving school unable to read and write is small; publishing is no longer a leisurely and gentlemanly job, but a rat-race business in which the accountant may be the supremo, caring little for books but much for profits; agents and authors' unions have gained recognition for the rights of authors, advice is freely to be found, and even those authors who do not have agents and who do not belong to the Society of Authors or the Writers' Guild have benefited from their activities and efforts. All this has meant that publishers' agreements have become long and complicated, and have mostly been drawn up by specialists, often trained in the law, who have been concerned to make them not only legally watertight, but fully comprehensive, so that they cover all the possible circumstances in which the author, the publisher and the book itself might find themselves.

It must be pointed out, however, that a simple letter can still be, and frequently is, regarded as a contract. Indeed, because of its simplicity it could be all-embracing. Moreover, letters attached to a formal contract, whether amending it or amplifying it, are considered as part of that agreement and have full legal standing as such. Even conversations over the telephone can be considered to be legally binding, as was proved in a recent case (but any author given an oral commitment by a publisher would be wise to put his understanding of the conversation into written form and to send a copy to the publisher with a request for written confirmation of its content).

Nevertheless, most authors are more likely to be faced with the formidable document which a publisher offers when he has decided to take on your book, and unless you are experienced in these matters you will almost certainly need to take advice before signing the agreement. It is not that you are in grave danger of being really badly treated – although you may still come across the occasional scoundrel, on the whole publishers are reasonably honest (even the few who are tempted to cheat may be restrained by the need to preserve their reputations) – but it is important always to understand what you are going to sign. If you have an agent you should be able to rely on his ability to vet the contract (he will, in fact, probably insist on using his own form of agreement, if he has one – though not all agents do); alternatively, if you belong to the Society of Authors or the Writers' Guild, you will be able to get help from them. However, it really is advisable to know something about the subject yourself, to understand the language commonly used in publishing agreements, to know when to accept without demur, when to argue gently, and when (quite often, because although most publishers won't cheat, they'll certainly not do themselves down) to dig your heels in.

This book is intended to give useful advice in all those areas.

It will also attempt to cover its subject as widely as possible, but inevitably will at times deal with generalities rather than specific cases. As publishers are wont to say whenever given the opportunity, all books are different, and because they are different, the terms under which they are published are different. And just as books are different, so are all publishers, and their contracts are not uniform. In other words, there is no such thing as a contract which is accepted throughout the trade, and when a publisher says to you, 'That is standard practice in the trade,' although, since publishers do not normally show each other their agreement forms, he may easily believe what he is saying, what is usually meant is merely that it is standard for his company.

Some years ago publishers had printed contract forms with spaces for the insertion of wording which might be applicable only to the book in question, and at least in most cases the already printed clauses were clearly standard to that publisher. Nowadays, contracts are produced on a word processor and there is no way of telling whether any of the terms are variations from the publisher's norm. (And, incidentally, since an individual contract is produced for each book, it is possible for errors and omissions to occur, so careful scrutiny is essential.)

You may also be told by the publisher that the agreement which has been drawn up is a 'boilerplate'. This term is mostly used in respect of contracts drawn up by agents. To save constant negotiation with publishers over basic provisions of the contract, the agent and the publisher have agreed on wording acceptable to both, and this is then regarded as 'a boilerplate' and used as a basis whenever that publisher signs up a new book from that agent. Whether the publisher talks of 'standard' or 'boilerplate' terms, it would be wise to let a little alarm bell ring in your mind – the fact that something is always done in a particular way is not always a strong claim to its acceptability.

In any case, you must always be on your guard. You are in a buyer's market – any publisher at any time can easily find large numbers of publishable books – so it is a case of *caveat venditor*, you being the *venditor*. If you are a member of the Society of Authors or the Writers' Guild and are offered a contract by a publisher who has signed the Minimum Terms Agreement (see Chapter 2), you can be reasonably certain that the agreement will be acceptable in most respects, but even in such cases you should read it with care and make sure that you understand it, and that there is nothing in it which you feel is unfair to you. If you are not a member of the Society or the Guild, or if you are dealing with a publisher who has not signed an MTA, you need to be extra careful.

As already mentioned, no two publishers are likely to have exactly similar agreements – they all cover almost all the same basic points, but the clauses usually come in different orders, and there is considerable variety in the wording. Contracts which are not based on the MTA are likely to contain terms which are not as good as might be hoped from the author's point of view, but there is no consistency in this – some agreements are better than others throughout, and you may even come across one which has, perhaps, a couple of clauses which seem remarkably generous towards the author. (Will it be considered over-cynical if I say that the generosity will probably be shown on the subsidiary rights which are least likely to be sold? In any case, always beware of something in your contract which seems particularly beneficent – it is almost invariably a sign that some of its other provisions will be quite iniquitous, and you might remember that saying about Greeks bearing gifts.)

Whatever the agreement is like, forget that it is about your baby, the book you have slaved over for months or years, and into which you have poured your heart and soul; forget that a publisher, to your astonished delight, has actually agreed to publish and sell the book, and is going to pay you hard cash as soon as you have signed the contract; instead, remember that this is a legal document, every comma of which needs to be checked – remember it even if you are an experienced author who has signed many contracts already – and use this book to help you find your way through the jungle.

I hope the book will have an additional use. To explain it, let us assume that you have received a contract from a publisher. You may think, especially if you are a delighted-to-be-accepted first-time author, that the agreement sets out the final, immutable terms on which the publisher is prepared to publish your book. It is not necessarily so, and in most cases it is in fact a negotiable document. You can question its terms, you can ask for changes, you can even refuse to sign unless certain clauses are removed altogether if you feel really strongly about them and are sure that you are justified in objecting to them. And you should not be afraid of these things. By the time that a publisher has drawn up a contract he has not only decided that he likes the book and wants to publish it, but he is pretty well committed to it and has already spent a considerable amount of time and trouble over it – and that does not apply only to the book which he sees as a potential bestseller, but to all the books which he takes on to his list. That being so, the fact that you dare to query points in the agreement or ask for improvement in the terms is not going to make him decide to abandon his plans for the book and to tear up the contract before it is even signed (provided that you put forward your questions and requests in a reasonable and polite way, so that you do not upset him on behavioural grounds). There are, of course, occasions when the commitment to the book is less strong than you might hope, and equally there are some publishers who work very strictly to their own standard terms and are unwilling to alter them – indeed, both these conditions may apply – but in such cases the publisher can always refuse your requests (although I believe he should be willing to discuss the matter and explain why he cannot make any changes). You then have to decide whether to give in and sign or refuse to do so and run the risk of not finding another publisher who is willing to take your book on. If you decide to sign, the publisher won't think any the worse of you or of your book because you had the temerity to question certain points in the contract.

The other use of this book, then, is to compare the

contract you have been offered with some of the other examples in this text, so that you can see perhaps what it is reasonable to question, and what is not. And I hope too that you
will take note of those paragraphs which have been headed
WARNING, in which I point out some of the things which
you may find in publishers' contracts which you should not
accept without demur.

I should also like to make it clear that even after you have
signed a contract, changes can be made. It *is* a legal document, it *is* enforceable, and if either party wants to stand firm
on its terms, it is possible for them to do so. But it can also be
altered if both parties agree, even though it was signed
weeks, months or years ago. So if there is something about
the contract you have signed with which you are not happy,
ask your publisher about it, and you may find that he will
agree to meet your objections, or perhaps you will be able to
reach some compromise situation. Publishers can be obdu-
rate, but most of them prefer to keep their authors happy if
they can.

2 The Minimum Terms Agreement

Ever since the invention of printing, authors have believed (often, but not always, with justification) that they are victims of the publishers' arrogance, greed and lack of scruples. This was the prime reason for the foundation, in 1884, of the Society of Authors. Since publishers were permanently in a buyer's market, except perhaps when dealing with a handful of authors who had exceptional clout because they were constantly in the bestseller lists, there was little that could be done. However, during the last forty years or so – decades which have seen a greater awareness than ever before of the rights of the individual – it became plain that authors were no longer content, despite the weakness of their position as vendors in what is still a buyer's market, to accept what they regarded as exploitation by publishers. In 1980 the two organizations which represent authors, the Society of Authors and the more recently formed Writers' Guild of Great Britain, produced a form of contract, which became known as the Minimum Terms Agreement (MTA).

To quote my own book, *An Author's Guide to Publishing*, 'in this document they set out not only to lay down standards on financial matters, such as the royalty rates and the various splits of subsidiary earnings which they considered acceptable, but also to allow authors the right to be kept informed of publishing plans for their books and to be consulted on such subjects as jackets, blurbs and publicity. The Society and the Guild jointly tried to persuade the Publishers Association to adopt the MTA on behalf of all its members. The PA predictably argued that it could not bind its individual members in any way, but drew up a "Code of Practice", to which it hoped they would adhere. The Code was both bland and unenforceable. The Society and the Guild then set about persuading individual publishing firms to sign the MTA.' Although comparatively few firms have so far signed the agreement, its influence has been considerable. One of the reasons why publishers do not, as a group, accept the MTA, and why the Publishers Association makes no attempt to impose any kind of uniformity on its members' contractual terms, is that all books are different, and many companies have refused to sign the MTA largely on the somewhat specious grounds that it does not allow them the essential freedom to negotiate widely-varying contracts according to the nature of the books and the markets concerned. However, many of even the most recalcitrant firms, under pressure from the Society and the Guild, from agents and from individual authors, have amended their standard agreements in order to bring them more in line with current attitudes and therefore with the MTA. It is worth noting, too, that the Society and the Guild continue to press leading houses to become signatories, and as each year passes are able to announce further successes.

The Minimum Terms Agreement is in fact a contract between two parties, one of which is the Society of Authors and the Writers' Guild jointly, and the other is a given publisher. It is not an agreement between a publisher and an author, but simply sets out the minimum financial terms and other conditions to be embodied in the agreements which the publisher concerned will offer *to authors who are members of the Society or of the Guild (or of both)*, so if you are not a member of either of those organizations, you may not benefit even if your publisher has signed (if you *are* a member you should let the publisher know before the agreement is drawn up). I believe, however, that some publishers who are signatories of the MTA, although they are not bound to do so, offer contracts based upon it to *all* their authors, whether or not they belong to either of the associations.

It seems to me useful to reprint in the following pages a version of the MTA because it will provide a useful starting point for a clause-by-clause discussion of the wording that you are likely to find in almost any publishing agreement. It should be remembered that, as in other matters, when it comes to signing the MTA, publishers like to retain their individuality, so the wording of each MTA differs, and some exclude certain points, while others may insist on the insertion of what might be considered an unusual clause. However, none of the variations is of major significance, since the Society and the Guild, while willing to negotiate and compromise on the wording and on matters which they believe to be of minor importance, will not sign a Minimum Terms Agreement unless it meets their basic requirements. The MTA which follows can therefore be described as typical, even if no other version is exactly the same.

Terms of the Contract between the Author and the Publisher as laid down in a typical version of the Minimum Terms Agreement

1. The Typescript and its Delivery

a) The contract shall specify full details of the work including its title, length, number and type of illustrations, index etc and may refer expressly to a synopsis, specified correspondence between the Publisher and the Author and any other relevant material submitted by the Author. There shall also be stated (without being binding on the Publisher) the number of copies the Publisher plans to print initially, the proposed format (i.e. hardback and/or paperback) and the anticipated retail price(s). In the case of commissioned works, the planned print run and anticipated retail price(s) may alternatively be disclosed on delivery of the typescript. The Author shall deliver by the date specified in the contract two legible copies of the typescript of the work, which shall be professionally competent and ready for press.

b) Within 30 days of delivery the Publisher shall notify the Author if any changes to the script are required (or if the script is to be rejected).
   Within a further 30 days (or such reasonable necessary longer period as may be notified to the Author) the Publisher shall specify the changes

required (or provide detailed reasons in writing for rejecting the script).

If the typescript is rejected because of the Author's failure to comply with Clause 1(a) he/she shall be liable to repay, if so requested, the part of the advance already received.

c)   Should the Author fail to meet the agreed delivery date, the Publisher may agree with the Author a later date or give the Author reasonable notice in writing to deliver the work and should he/she fail to do so the Publisher shall be entitled to terminate the contract in which event the part of the advance received shall be returnable and all rights shall revert to the Author.

2. Warranty and Indemnity

The Author shall warrant:

(i)   that the work is original, that he/she is the owner thereof and free to contract, and that the work has not previously been published in volume form elsewhere; and

(ii)   that the work will not contain anything that infringes copyright or is libellous or obscene or otherwise unlawful; nor will it infringe third parties' rights; and

(iii) that all statements purporting to be facts are true and that any recipe, information, formula or instructions contained therein will not, if the reader were reasonably to act thereupon, cause injury, illness or any damage to the user or third parties.

The Author shall indemnify the Publisher against costs, expenses, loss and damage resulting from any breach of the foregoing warranties or any claim alleging breach thereof (excluding any claims which are reasonably deemed by the Publisher to be groundless, vexatious or purely malicious). The indemnity shall survive termination of the contract.

The Publisher reserves the right to request the Author to alter or amend the text of the work in such a way as may appear to the Publisher appropriate for the purpose of removing any passage which on the advice of the Publisher's legal advisers (in association with the Author's legal advisers, if he/she so wishes) may be considered objectionable or likely to be actionable at law, but any such alteration or removal shall be without prejudice to and shall not affect the Author's liability under the warranties and indemnity on his/her part. If the Author declines in such circumstances to alter or amend the text, the Publisher reserves the right to terminate the contract and seek reimbursement of the advance.

3. Copyright Fees and Index

a) The Publisher shall pay any copyright fees for agreed illustrations, unless otherwise agreed (in which event the Publisher will contribute at least £250). The responsibility for clearing and paying for quotations shall be a matter for individual negotiation.

b) If in the opinion of the Author and the Publisher an index is required, but the Author does not wish to undertake the task, the Publisher shall engage a competent indexer to do so and the costs shall be shared equally between the Author and the Publisher, the Author's share being deducted from money due to the Author.

4. Licence and Review

a) The copyright in the work shall remain the property of the Author who shall grant to the Publisher the sole and exclusive right for a period of 20 years from the date of first publication ("the initial term") to print, publish and sell the work in volume form in the English language (or in any language as the case may be) in the territories specified in the contract and to sub-license such rights specified in clauses 15, 16, 17 and 18 hereof as may be agreed in the contract. The Publisher will inform the Author of all sub-licences granted (excluding anthology and quotation rights) and supply copies thereof on request. In particular the Author will be fully consulted and have an adequate opportunity to discuss and comment (without undue delay) on all proposed major sub-licences (including but not limited to serial, paperback, American, film, television and merchandising deals).

b) On every tenth anniversary of the publication date (or within a reasonable time thereafter) either party may give written notice to the other that it wishes specified terms in the contract to be reviewed, in which case those terms shall be considered in the light of comparable terms then prevailing in the trade and shall be altered (with effect from the date of the notice) to the extent that may be just and equitable. Failing agreement on what may be just and equitable the matter shall be referred to arbitration under clause 27.

c) If the work is in print (as defined herein) at the end of 17 years from the first publication, the Publisher may inform the Author in writing of the date that the contract is due to expire and invite the Author (or his/her executors, as the case may be) to negotiate in good faith with the intention of reaching agreement on revised terms for a further period. The Author, if so requested by the Publisher, shall inform the Publisher of the terms offered (if any) by other publishers and the Publisher shall be given an opportunity to match such terms but the final decision shall rest with the Author.

d) If, with the Author's consent (such consent not to be unreasonably withheld), a licence is granted by the Publisher extending beyond the initial term, the reversion of rights to the Author (if applicable) shall be without prejudice to the continuation of that licence and the Publisher's entitlement to the Publisher's share of the proceeds therefrom. But the Publisher shall not be entitled to extend or renew, without the Author's consent, any licence granted which is due to terminate after the initial term (unless and until a further agreement is reached under (c) above).

5. The Publisher's Undertaking to Publish

The Publisher shall publish the work at the Publisher's own expense and risk within 12 months (unless there are particular reasons for later publication or unless the Publisher is prevented from so publishing by circumstances beyond its control) of delivery of the typescript and any other material specified in the contract. Should the Publisher decline to publish the work for any reason other than the Author's failure to meet the specifications in clause 1(a), the advance stipulated in clause 9 (including any balance unpaid) shall be paid to the Author without prejudice to any additional compensation to which he/she may be entitled for breach of contract.

6. Production

a) All details as to the manner of production and publication and the number and destination of free copies shall be under the control of the Publisher who undertakes to produce the book to a high standard.

b) The Publisher shall consult the Author and obtain his/her approval on copy editing and the final number and type of illustrations (unless, because of the topicality of the book, time does not permit), such approval not to be unreasonably withheld or delayed. The Publisher shall consult the Author about publication date. The Author shall be shown artists' roughs (or, if that is impracticable, proofs) of the jacket and shall be fully consulted thereon and on the blurb in good time before publication, but the final decision shall be the Publisher's.

c) No changes in the title or text (other than changes

made to conform to the Publisher's house style) shall be made by the Publisher without the Author's consent, such consent not to be unreasonably withheld.

d)   In ample time before publication the Author shall be sent a questionnaire inviting him/her to supply personal information relevant to publicity and marketing, to suggest who should receive review/free copies and to say whether he/she wishes the typescript to be returned.

e)   The Publisher will disclose to the Author, on request, the size of the first and subsequent print runs.

f)   Within thirty days of publication the Publisher shall return to the Author the typescript of the work, if so requested.

g)   The Publisher shall ensure that the provisions contained in (c) above are included in any contract for sub-licensed editions of the work.

7. Approval of Final Edited Script and Correction of Proofs

a)   Unless the Author has already seen a copy of the edited typescript or does not wish to see it, he/she shall be sent a copy for approval – normally at least 10 working days before it goes to the printers – and he/she shall respond as soon as possible.

b)   The Author shall be sent two complete sets of proofs of the work. The Author shall correct and return one set of proofs to the Publisher within 15 working days (or such other period as may be agreed). The Author shall bear the cost of proof corrections (other than printers' or publisher's errors) in excess of 15% of the cost of composition, such cost to be deducted from the advance or royalties.

8. Copyright Notice and Credit to the Author

A copyright notice in the form © followed by the Author's name and the year of first publication shall be printed on all copies of the work and the Author's name shall appear prominently on the jacket, binding and title page of the work and in all publicity material. The Publisher shall ensure that an identical copyright notice appears in all sub-licensed editions of the work.

9. Advance

a) Unless the Author requests a lower figure, the Publisher shall pay the Author an advance against royalties and earnings of not less than the following percentage of the Author's estimated receipts from the sale of the projected first printing:
  (i) 65% if the work is to be published by the Publisher only in hardback or only in paperback
  (ii) 55% if the work is to be published by the Publisher in both hardback and paperback.
b) In the case of a non-commissioned work half the advance shall be paid on signature of the contract and half within one year of signature or on publication, whichever is the sooner (or as may be otherwise agreed at the Author's request).
c) In the case of a commissioned work the advance shall be paid one third on signature of the contract, one third on delivery of the final and revised typescript and one third within one year of delivery of the typescript or on publication whichever is the sooner (or as may otherwise be agreed at the Author's request).
d) The provisions of (b) and (c) may be varied by agreement when the work is to be published first in hardback and then in paperback under the Publisher's own imprint.

10. Hardback Royalties

a) ON HOME MARKET SALES IN THE UK AND IRISH REPUBLIC
10% of the British published price on the first 2,500

copies, 12½% on the next 2,500 copies, and 15% thereafter except on works for children when the royalty will be 7½% rising to 10% after 3,000 copies. [In exceptional circumstances involving long works of fiction being published in short print-runs for libraries or works of drama or poetry being published in short print-runs, the Publisher may wish to ask the Author to consider accepting a lower starting royalty for specified reasons.]

b) ON OVERSEAS SALES
10% of the price received on the first 2,500 copies, 12½% on the next 2,500 copies and 15% thereafter, except on works for children when the royalty will be 7½% rising to 10% after 3,000 copies. If the work is published abroad in a separate local edition, royalties will be paid at a rate to be mutually agreed on the local published price.

c) ON REPRINTS OF 1,500 COPIES OR LESS
The royalties shall revert to the starting royalties, except that the Publisher may not invoke this provision more than once in twelve months without prior agreement of the Author.

d) CHEAP AND OTHER HARDBACK EDITIONS
The Publisher shall pay to the Author a royalty to be agreed on any hardback edition published at less than two-thirds of the original published price, on any "special" hardback edition under the Publisher's imprint (e.g. an educational or large print edition), and on any other edition not covered by (a) or (b) above.

11. Paperbacks

a) Should the Publisher publish a paperback edition under one of the Publisher's own imprints the Publisher shall pay to the Author on home sales 7½% of the British published price on the first

50,000 copies and 10% thereafter. On works for children, the Publisher shall pay 5% to 10,000 copies and 7½% thereafter. The royalty on copies sold for export shall be 6% of the British published price (4% in the case of works for children). If the work is published abroad in a separate local edition, royalties will be at a rate to be agreed based on the local published price.

b) Should the Publisher sub-license paperback rights to an independent paperback publisher, all moneys accruing under such sub-licences shall be divided in the proportion 60% to the Author 40% to the Publisher up to a point to be negotiated and then 70%:30% thereafter.

12. Returns

The Publisher shall have the right to set aside as a reserve against returns 10% (h/b)/20% (p/b) of the royalties earned on the first royalty statement (after first publication or reissue) and to withhold this sum up to and including the second (h/b)/third (p/b) royalty statement, following which all moneys shall be paid in full and the Publisher shall accept responsibility for any overpayments resulting from subsequent returns.

13. Remainders and Surplus Stock

If the Publisher wishes
a) To sell copies at a reduced price or as a remainder, the Author will be given the option to purchase copies at the remainder price and will be paid 5% of the net receipts of other sales;
b) To destroy surplus bound copies, the Publisher will notify him/her accordingly and the Author shall have the right to obtain free copies within 20 working days of the notification.
There shall be no disposals under this clause within one year of first publication.

14. Royalty Free Copies

No royalties shall be paid on copies given away free to the Author or others, review or returned copies, or those destroyed by fire, water, in transit or otherwise.

15. Bookclub Rights

Should the Publisher sub-license simultaneous or reprint bookclub rights the Publisher shall pay the Author as follows:
a) On bound copies or sheets sold to the bookclub: 10% of receipts.
b) On copies manufactured by the bookclub: 60% of the Publisher's receipts.

16. United States Rights

If the Author grants to the Publisher US rights in the work, the Publisher shall make every effort:
either to arrange the publication of an American edition of the work on a royalty basis, in which case the Publisher shall retain not more than 15% of the proceeds inclusive of any sub-agent's commission;
or to sell bound copies, in which case the Publisher will endeavour whenever reasonably possible to see that the Author is paid royalties (the percentage(s) to be agreed) related to the US published price. If the Publisher is unable or does not consider it reasonably possible to secure a royalty, the Publisher shall offer copies or sheets for sale inclusive of royalty, in which case the Author will be paid 15% of the Publisher's receipts, unless the discount is 60% or more in which case the Author will be paid 10% of the Publisher's receipts.

17. Translation Rights

If the Author grants to the Publisher translation rights in the work, the Publisher shall retain not more than 20% of the proceeds from any foreign language edition inclusive of any sub-agent's commission.

18. Subsidiary Rights

a) The Publisher shall pay to the Author the following percentages of the proceeds (after the deduction of any sub-agent's commission in the case of merchandising) from the licensing of the following rights:

(i)	Second (i.e. post volume publication) serial rights	75% *
(ii)	Anthology & quotation rights	50%
(iii)	Condensation rights – magazines	75%
	– books	50%
(iv)	Strip cartoon rights	75% *
(v)	TV, radio and recorded readings	75% *
(vi)	Merchandising	80% *
(vii)	One shot periodical	75%
(viii)	Hardcover reprint, loose leaf, and large print	50%

* These rights may or may not be granted to the Publisher according to the terms of the contract. If necessary, the Author will, at the Publisher's request, join in the granting of any such rights.

b) If the Publisher wishes to act as agent for the sale of any of the following rights (for which there is no collective licensing scheme) and the Author so agrees, the Publisher shall pay 90% of the net proceeds to the Author:
First serial rights, TV and radio dramatisation, film and dramatic rights and electronic publishing rights. Any legal fees or professional charges incurred directly in connection with the sale of film or video rights will be charged against the gross income.

c) Reprographic rights shall be granted by the Author and the Publisher to the ALCS and PLS respectively.

Any other income from reprography not covered by collective licensing schemes shall be handled by the Publisher and the income divided 50:50. In relation to editions of the work published by the Publisher, these provisions shall survive the termination of the contract.

d) Public Lending Right and all other rights not specified above shall be reserved by the Author.

19. Author's Copies

The Author shall receive on publication 12 free copies of the work and shall have the right to purchase further copies for personal use at 50% discount if payment accompanies the order or 35% discount if credit is to be extended to the Author or if the amount is to be charged to the Author's royalty account. Should a paperback edition be issued under clause 11(a), the Author shall be entitled to 20 free copies. If the work has more than one author, the free copies shall be divided accordingly.

20. Accounts

a) The Publisher shall make up accounts at six monthly intervals and shall render such accounts and pay all moneys due to the Author within three months thereof.

b) Any sum of £100 or more due to the Author in respect of sub-licensed rights shall be paid to the Author within one month of receipt provided the advance has been earned.

c) Each statement of account shall contain at least as much information as is given in the Model Royalty Statement agreed between the Publishers Association and the Society of Authors. In particular print runs and opening and closing stock figures will be stated. The Publisher shall supply copies of statements received from sub-licensees, unless such statements contain information about other authors in which case information will be provided on request.

d) The Author or his/her authorised representative shall have the right upon written request to examine the Publisher's books of account (during normal working hours) in so far as they relate to the work, which examination shall be at the cost of the Author unless errors exceeding £50 shall be found to his/her disadvantage in which case the costs shall be paid by the Publisher.

21. Actions for Infringement

a) It is agreed that if the Publisher considers that the copyright or any one or more of the Publisher's exclusive licences in the work has been infringed and the Author after receiving written notice of such infringement from the Publisher refuses or neglects to take adequate proceedings in respect of the infringement, the Publisher shall be at liberty to take such steps as the Publisher considers necessary for dealing with the matter and if the Publisher desires to take proceedings shall be entitled to do so in the joint names of the Publisher and the Author upon giving the Author a sufficient and reasonable security to indemnify the Author against any liability for costs and in this event any sum received by way of damages shall belong to the Publisher. If the Author is willing to take proceedings and the Publisher desires to be joined with him/her as a party thereto and agrees to share the costs then if any sum is recovered by way of damages and costs such sum shall be applied in payment of the costs incurred and the balance shall be divided between the Author and the Publisher in proportion to the Author's and the Publisher's shares of the costs.

b) The provisions of this clause are intended only to apply in the case of an infringement of the copyright in the work affecting the interest in the same granted to the Publisher under the contract.

22. Revised Editions

If the Publisher and the Author agree that the work should be revised in order to bring it up to date, the Author, subject if reasonable to the payment of an agreed advance, will undertake such revision. In the event of the Author being unable by reason of death or otherwise to edit or revise the work, the Publisher may procure some other person to edit or revise the work and, subject to the approval of the Author or his/her executors, such approval not to be unreasonably withheld, may deduct the expense thereof from all moneys payable to the Author under the contract.

23. Assignment

The Publisher shall not assign the rights granted to the Publisher in the contract or the benefit thereof without the Author's written consent (such consent not to be unreasonably withheld).

24. Termination

a) If the Publisher fails to fulfil or comply with any of the provisions of the contract within one month after notification from the Author of such failure or if the Publisher goes into liquidation (except a voluntary liquidation for the purpose of reconstruction) or has a Receiver appointed, the contract shall automatically terminate and all rights shall revert to the Author.

b) When all editions of the work published by the Publisher are out of print the Author may give notice in writing inviting the Publisher to decide whether or not to reprint or reissue the work. Within six weeks the Publisher shall notify the Author in writing:

    (i)   that the Publisher does not intend to reprint or reissue the work, in which case the contract shall terminate automatically and all rights

granted shall revert to the Author when stocks
are exhausted or within 6 months whichever
shall be the sooner; or
(ii) that the Publisher will reprint or reissue the
work, in which case the Publisher shall do so
within eight months of receiving the notice from
the Author; or
(iii) that the Publisher wishes to issue a revised
edition, in which case the provisions of clause 22
will apply.

The work shall be considered out of print if fewer than
50 copies of the hardback and 150 copies of the
paperback remain in stock (as to which the Publisher
will inform the Author). The rights shall not revert
until any money owed by the Author to the Publisher
has been paid.

c) Termination under (a) or (b) shall be without prejudice to:
(i) any sub-licences properly granted by the
Publisher during the currency of the contract,
and
(ii) any income due to the Publisher if termination is
under (b) above, and
(iii) any claims which the Author may have for
moneys due at the time of such termination, and
(iv) any claims which the Author may have against
the Publisher in respect of breaches by the
Publisher of the terms of the contract.

25. Advertisements

The Publisher shall not insert within the work or on its
cover or dust jacket any advertisement other than for its
own works without the Author's consent and shall use its
best endeavours to see that a similar condition is contained in all sub-licences.

26. First Refusal

The Publisher may ask the Author for first refusal on his/her next work, in which case the Publisher will make any offer for the next work within three weeks of receipt of a synopsis or within six weeks of receipt of a complete typescript as the case may be.

27. Moral Rights

The Publisher shall observe the moral rights conferred on the Author under the Copyright, Designs and Patents Act 1988. The Author's right of paternity shall be "asserted" in the manner recommended by the Society of Authors and the Writers' Guild.

28. Disputes

Any dispute arising in connection with the contract, which shall be interpreted in accordance with the law of England, shall be referred to a single agreed referee on terms to be agreed between the parties informally. Failing agreement about the appointment of a suitable referee the matter shall become subject to arbitration in accordance with the Arbitration Act 1950 or any amending or substituted statute for the time being in force.

WARNING

The example of a Minimum Terms Agreement quoted above may be taken as typical – and typically it is not perfect. Detailed comments on wording which might be improved will be given in Chapter 4, *An Analysis of British Hardcover Publishers' Agreements*. The points at issue are contained in sub-clause iii of Clause 2 'Warranty and Indemnity' (see comments on p. 72), in sub-clause c of Clause 10 'Hardback Royalties' (see p. 99), in sub-clause *a* of Clause 13 'Remainders and Surplus Stock' (see p. 114 and 115), in sub-clause *d* of Clause 20 'Accounts' (see p. 120–1), and in sub-clauses *a, b* and *c* of Clause 24 'Termination' (see pp. 124–6).

It is perhaps worth noting that although the MTA is designed to give authors a better deal from their publishers, it also imposes some burdens on them, by spelling out their obligations more firmly than may sometimes be the case in non-MTA-type contracts. It is, of course, reasonable that publishers who are asked to improve their terms and their attitudes towards authors should want in return a more professional standard of behaviour from their authors than has often been seen in the past. A partnership, which is the ideal relationship for the two parties to a publishing agreement, demands a sense of responsibility on both sides.

3 The Publishers Association Code of Practice

When the Society of Authors and the Writers' Guild first drew up the Minimum Terms Agreement in 1980 (a much more militant version, incidentally, than those which individual publishers have signed since that time), they tried to persuade the Publishers Association to adopt it as a form to which all their members would adhere. The PA refused – not, they said, necessarily because the terms were unacceptable, but because the structure of their organization did not allow them to impose conditions of any sort on their members. However, in 1982 the PA produced a Code of Practice. It has no binding force on any PA member, let alone the many firms (some of them major concerns) which do not belong to the Association. Nevertheless, it marks a step forward in author/publisher relationships and must therefore be given one cheer, if not the preferred three.

By kind permission of the Publishers Association, the latest version of the Code of Practice is printed below.

The Publishers Association Code of Practice

A constructive and co-operative relationship between authors (and the agents and representatives acting for them) and their publishers is vital to successful publishing. In the great majority of cases this relationship undoubtedly exists. Nevertheless, there can be dissatisfaction, perhaps because a title is not the success the author and publisher hoped for but also because of misunderstandings of the publishing contract, uncertainties and poor drafting, and 'customs of trade' unappreciated by the author.

The Council of the Publishers Association believes that everything possible should be done to ensure a satisfactory relationship and avoid disputes. It has therefore prepared the Code of Practice for book publishers set out below, which it recommends to members in their dealings with authors. This Code gives guidance only. It cannot deal with every variation. In general, however, failure to accept the guidance in the Code without good reason is clearly likely to damage the standing of individual publishers and of publishing generally.

Book publishing is so varied in its scope that contracts are likely to contain many variations between, for example, different types of book with different markets, different degrees of editorial involvement by the publisher, and established or relatively new authors. Total uniformity of contract or practice is therefore impracticable. In particular, some academic, educational and reference books and works based on a variety of contributions may be subject to special considerations, though the necessity to follow the general principles of this Code remains.

NB. This Code of Practice applies only to agreements whereby an author assigns or licenses an interest in the copyright of a work to a publisher, and does not apply to agreements whereby an author invests money in the publication of a work.

1. The publishing contract must be clear, unambiguous and comprehensive, and must be honoured in both the letter and the spirit.

Matters which particularly need to be defined in the contract include:–

    (i) a title which identifies the work or (for incomplete works) the nature and agreed length and scope of the work.

    (ii) the nature of the rights conferred – the ownership of the copyright (an assignment or an exclusive licence), whether all volume rights (or part of the volume rights or more than volume rights) and the territories and languages covered.

    (iii) the time scale for delivery of the manuscript and for publication.

(iv) the payments, royalties and advances (if any) to be paid, what they are in respect of and when they are due.

(v) the provisions for sub-licensing.

(vi) the responsibility for preparing the supporting materials (e.g. indexes, illustrations, etc.) in which the author holds the copyright and for obtaining permissions and paying for the supporting materials in which the copyright is held by third parties.

(vii) the termination and reversion provisions of the contract.

Should the parties subsequently agree changes to the contract, these should be recorded in writing between them.

2. The author should retain ownership of the copyright, unless there are good reasons otherwise.

An exclusive licence should be sufficient to enable the publisher to exploit and protect most works effectively. In particular fields of publishing (e.g. encyclopaedic and reference works, certain types of academic works, publishers' compilations edited from many outside contributions, some translations and works particularly vulnerable to copyright infringement because of their extensive international sale) it may be appropriate for the copyright to be vested in the publisher.

3. The publisher should ensure that an author who is not professionally represented has a proper opportunity for explanation of the terms of the contract and the reasons for each provision.

4. The contract must set out reasonable and precise terms for the reversion of rights.

When a publisher has invested in the development of an author's work on the market, and the work is a contribution to the store of literature and knowledge, and the publisher expects to market the work actively for many years, it is reasonable to acquire volume rights for the full term of copyright, on condition that there are safeguards providing for reversion in appropriate circumstances.

The circumstances under which the grant of rights

acquired by the publisher will revert to the author (e.g.
fundamental breach of contract by the publisher, or when a
title has been out of print or has not been available on the
market for a stipulated time) should form a part of the
formal contract. In addition, a reversion of particular rights
that either have never been successfully exploited by the
publisher, or which are not subject to any current (or
immediately anticipated) licence or edition, may, after a
reasonable period from their first acquisition and after
proper notice, be returned on request to the author,
provided that such partial reversions do not adversely affect
other retained rights (e.g. the absence of an English-
language edition should not affect the licensing publisher's
interest in a translated edition still in print) and provided
that payments made by the publisher to or on behalf of the
author have been earned.

**5. The publisher must give the author a proper opportunity to
share in the success of the work.**
In general, the publishing contract should seek to achieve a
fair balance of reward for author and publisher. On occasion
it may be appropriate, when the publisher is taking an
exceptional risk in publishing a work, or the origination
costs are unusually high, for the author to assist the
publication of the work by accepting initially a low royalty
return. In such cases, it is also appropriate for the publisher
to agree that the author should share in success by, for
example, agreeing that the royalty rates should increase to
reflect that success.
If under the contract the author receives an outright or
single payment, but retains ownership of the copyright, the
publisher should be prepared to share with the author any
income derived from a use of the work not within the
reasonable contemplation of the parties at the time of the
contract.

**6. The publisher must handle manuscripts promptly, and
keep the author informed of progress.**
All manuscripts and synopses received by the publisher,
whether solicited or unsolicited, should be acknowledged as
soon as received. The author may be told at that time when

to expect to hear further, but in the absence of any such indication at least a progress report should be sent by the publisher to the author within six weeks of receipt. A longer time may be required in the case of certain works – e.g. those requiring a fully detailed assessment, particularly in cases where the opinion of specialist readers may not be readily available, and in planned co-editions – but the author should be informed of a likely date when a report may be expected.

Note: It is important for the publisher to know if the manuscript or synopsis is being simultaneously submitted to any other publisher.

7. The publisher must not cancel a contract without good and proper reason.
It is not easy to define objectively what constitutes unsuitability for publication of a commissioned manuscript or proper cause for the cancellation of a contract, since these may depend on a variety of circumstances. In any such case, however, the publisher must give the author sufficiently detailed reasons for rejection.

When the publisher requires changes in a commissioned manuscript as a condition of publication, these should be clearly set out in writing.

Note: In the case of unsolicited manuscripts or synopses, the publisher is under no obligation to give reasons for rejection, and is entitled to ask the author for return postage.
Time
If an author fails to deliver a completed manuscript according to the contract or within the contracted period, the publisher may be entitled (*inter alia*) to a refund of moneys advanced on account. However, it is commonly accepted that (except where time is of the essence) moneys advanced are not reclaimable until the publisher has given proper notice of intent to cancel the contract within a reasonable period from the date of such notice. Where the advance is not reclaimed after the period of notice has expired, it is reasonable for the publisher to retain an option to publish the work.
Standard and Quality
If an author has produced the work in good faith and with proper care, in accordance with the terms of the contract, but

the publisher decides not to publish on the grounds of quality, the publisher should not expect to reclaim on cancellation that part of any advance that has already been paid to the author. If, by contrast, the work has not been produced in good faith and with proper care, or the work does not conform to what has been commissioned, the publisher may be able to reclaim the advance.

Defamation and Illegality
The publisher is under no obligation to publish a work that there is reason to believe is defamatory or otherwise illegal.

Change of Circumstance
A change in the publisher's circumstances or policies is not a sufficient reason for declining to publish a commissioned work without compensation.

Compensation
Depending on the grounds for rejection,
   (i) the publisher may be liable for further advances due and an additional sum may be agreed to compensate the author, or
   (ii) the author may be liable to repay the advances received.

In the former case, the agreement for compensation may include an obligation on the author to return advances and compensation paid (or part of them) if the work is subsequently placed elsewhere.

Resolution of Disputes
Ideally, terms will be agreed privately between the parties, but in cases of dispute the matter should be put to a mutually agreed informal procedure, or if this cannot be agreed, to arbitration or normal legal procedures.

8. The contract must set out the anticipated timetable for publication.
The formal contract must make clear the time scale within which the author undertakes to deliver the complete manuscript, and within which the publisher undertakes to publish it. It should be recognised that in particular cases there may be valid reasons for diverging from these stated times, or for not determining strict time scales, and each party should be willing to submit detailed reasons for the agreement of the other party, if these should occur.

9. The publisher should be willing to share precautions against legal risks not arising from carelessness by the author.
For example:
Libel
While it remains the primary responsibility of the author to ensure that the work is not libellous – and particularly that it cannot be arraigned as a malicious libel – the publisher may also be liable. Libel therefore demands the closest co-operation between authors and publishers, in particular in sharing the costs of reading for libel and of any insurance considered to be desirable by the parties.

10. The publisher should consider helping the author by funding additional costs involved in preparing the work for publication.
If under contract the author is liable to pay for supporting materials, e.g. for permissions to use other copyright material, for the making and use of illustrations and maps, for costs of indexing, etc., the publisher may be willing to fund such expenses, to an agreed ceiling, that could reasonably be recovered against any such moneys as may subsequently become due to the author.

11. The publisher must ensure that the author receives a regular and clear account of sales made and moneys due.
The period during which sales are to be accounted for should be defined in the contract and should be followed, after a period also to be laid down in the contract, by a royalty statement and a remittance of moneys due. Publishers should always observe these dates and obligations scrupulously. Accounts should be rendered at least annually, and in the first year of publication the author may reasonably expect an intermediate statement and settlement. The initial pattern of sales of some educational books, however, may make such intermediate payment impracticable.

The current model royalty statement (1979) issued by the Association of Authors' Agents, the Society of Authors and the Writers' Guild, or the information suggested by it, should be used as a guide, and details of the statement should be adequately explained.

The publisher should pay the author on request the

appropriate share of any substantial advances received from major sub-licensing agreement by the end of the month following the month of receipt (providing moneys already advanced have been earned, and proper allowance made for returned stock; allowance may also need to be made if very substantial advances have been outstanding for an extended period of time).

The publisher should be prepared, on request, to disclose details of the number of copies printed, on condition that the author (and the agent) agree not to disclose the information to any other party.

Publishers should be prepared to give authors indications of sales to date, which must be realistic bearing in mind either unsold stock which may be returned by booksellers or stock supplied on consignment.

12. The publisher must ensure that the author can clearly ascertain how any payments due from sub-licensed agreements will be calculated.

Agreements under which the calculation of the author's share of any earnings is dependent on the publisher's allocation of direct costs and overheads can result in dissatisfaction unless the system of accounting is clearly defined.

13. The publisher should keep the author informed of important design, promotion, marketing and sub-licensing decisions.

Under the contract, final responsibility for decisions on the design, promotion and marketing of a book is normally vested in the publisher. Nevertheless, the fullest reasonable consultation with the author on such matters is generally desirable, both as a courtesy and in the interest of the success of the book itself. In particular the author should, if interested and available, be consulted about the proposed jacket, jacket copy and major promotional and review activities, be informed in advance of publication date and receive advance copies by that date. When time permits, the publisher should consult the author about the disposition of major sub-leases, and let the author have a copy of the agreement on request.

14. The integrity of the author's work should always be protected.
The author is entitled to ensure that the editorial integrity of the work is maintained. No significant alterations to the work (i.e. alterations other than those which could not reasonably be objected to) should be made without the author's consent, particularly where the author has retained the copyright.

The author who has retained ownership of the copyright is entitled also to be credited with the authorship of the work, and to retain ownership of the manuscript.

15. The publisher should inform the author clearly about opportunities for amendment of the work in the course of production.
The economics of printing make the incorporation of textual revisions after the book has been set extremely expensive. Publishers should always make it clear to authors, before a manuscript is put in hand, whether proofs are to be provided or not, on whom the responsibility for reading them rests and what scale of author's revisions would be acceptable to the publisher. If proofs are not being provided, the author should have the right to make final corrections to the copy-edited typescript, and the publisher should take responsibility for accurately reproducing this corrected text in type.

16. It is essential that both the publisher and the author have a clear common understanding of the significance attaching to the option clause in a publishing contract.
The option on an author's work can be of great importance to both parties. Options should be carefully negotiated, and the obligations that they impose should be clearly stated and understood on both sides. Option clauses covering more than one work may be undesirable, and should only be entered into with particular care.

17. The publisher should recognise that the remaindering of stock may effectively end the author's expectation of earnings.
Before a title is remaindered, the publisher should inform the author and offer all or part of the stock to the author on the

terms expected from the remainder dealer. Whether any royalty, related to the price received on such sales, should be paid is a matter to be determined by the publisher and the author at the time of the contract.

18. The publisher should endeavour to keep the author informed of changes in the ownership of the publishing rights and of any changes in the imprint under which a work appears. Most publishers will expect to sign their contracts on behalf of their successors and assigns, just as most authors will sign on behalf of their executors, administrators and assigns. But if changes in rights ownership or of publishing imprint subsequently occur, a publisher should certainly inform and, if at all possible, accommodate an author in these new circumstances.

19. The publisher should be willing to help the author and the author's estate in the administration of literary affairs. For example, the publisher should agree to act as an expert witness in questions relating to the valuation of a literary estate.

20. Above all, the publisher must recognise the importance of co-operation with the author in an enterprise in which both are essential. This relationship can be fulfilled only in an atmosphere of confidence, in which authors get the fullest possible credit for their work and achievements.
Note: This Code of Practice applies only to agreements whereby an author assigns or licenses an interest in the copyright of a work to a publisher, and does not apply to agreements whereby an author invests money in the publication of a work.
(The Code of Practice is Copyright © The Publishers Association 1982)

Any reader of this book who compares the Publishers Association Code of Practice with the Minimum Terms Agreement will notice many differences. Despite the protestations in the final clause of the Code, it is clear that the PA still regards authors as the junior partners in the enterprise, and throughout the Code some authors may feel that there is a sense of concessions being granted by the publishers out of the bigness of their hearts rather than in recognition that authors have a right to be rewarded and consulted and, in short, treated as equals. It might be possible to look upon the Code of Practice with more benevolence if one could be sure that all the members of the PA were adhering to it. But you have only to talk to any group of aspiring authors to provoke a bitter laugh, for instance, at the idea that publishers will give a verdict on books submitted to them within six weeks – 'more like six months,' they will say – and that would not be the only clause to evoke derision. As for that introductory paragraph with the suggestion that 'in the great majority of cases this (constructive and co-operative) relationship undoubtedly exists', the members of the PA should be flies on the wall at any authors' meeting, when they would learn that the vast majority of authors look upon publishers, alas, as The Enemy.

However, as I said earlier, the fact that publishers have made an attempt to meet the complaints of authors by producing this Code of Practice is something to welcome, even if it is flawed. At least when the Code was drawn up it showed that they had begun to listen. At least it showed that they could move from the rigid attitudes which had prevailed for most of this century. And although the PA has not produced a revised version of the Code since 1982, many publishers have since then progressed in some respects beyond it. Having begun to listen, and having moved a little, they will surely continue the process.

4   An Analysis of British Hardcover Publishers' Agreements

Introduction

Before beginning this clause-by-clause analysis of typical agreements used by hardcover publishers for a book consisting primarily of text, such as a novel, a biography, or a book like this one, which I suppose might be called a manual, it is important to point out that the general principles apply to other kinds of books and other kinds of publishing houses. If the publisher of your book is a paperback concern (in which case your book will probably be appearing as a paperback 'original' – i.e. a book which has not previously appeared in a hardcover edition), the agreement which you are offered is likely to contain all the same clauses as those which a hardcover publisher would offer. The one exception is that the paperback house will substitute the right to license others to produce a hardcover edition for the right to license others to produce a paperback edition.

Equally, highly illustrated books whether for children or adults, text books, and books with several authors, all of which are excluded from the Minimum Terms Agreement, should also follow the basic tenets of the hardcover agreement which is about to be analysed, though there may be major differences in royalty scales and various other matters. Further material on such books will be found in later chapters.

The layout and sequence of clauses differ in all publishers' agreements. For the purposes of this analysis I have divided the typical clauses into four groups, and these are:

The Preamble and the Grant of Rights – the introductory material at the beginning of the agreement and the clauses which define the rights, including subsidiary rights, which the agreement covers.

The Author's Obligations – Delivery of the Typescript; Illustrations and other Copyright Material; Index; Revised Editions; Warranty; Proofs; Publicity and Promotion; the Author's Use of his Own Material; Options.

The Publisher's Obligations – Publication; Consultation; Copyright Notice; Moral Rights; Consultation, Copyright Notice and Moral Rights in Sub-Licences; Advance; Royalties; Returns; Royalty-free Copies; Royalty and other Payments resulting from the sale of Subsidiary Rights; Paperback Rights; Hardcover Rights; Bookclub Rights; US Rights; Remainders; Author's Copies; Return of Author's Typescript; Accounts.

Other Clauses – Termination and Reversion of Rights; Actions for Infringement; Insurance; Trade Marks; Advertisements in Books; Arbitration; English Law; Income Tax; Agency; Headings; Signatories.

I   THE PREAMBLE AND THE GRANT OF RIGHTS

All formal publishing agreements begin with wording which defines the document as an agreement which has been made on a given date between the publisher and the author(s). This is known as the preamble – something which comes before the detail of what is actually agreed. No preamble was shown in the Minimum Terms Agreement printed in Chapter 2 because the MTA is not itself an agreement between a publisher and an author, but an agreement about the terms to be offered to the author by the publisher; its own preamble, which I did not include, refers to the Society of Authors and the Writers' Guild on the one hand and to the publisher concerned on the other.

The preamble in publishers' agreements takes a number of forms, but they are all variations on a theme, and it does not make much difference whether the first words are 'Memorandum of Agreement made this   day of 19 ' (the most frequently used opening) or whether it simply calls itself 'Agreement' or whether it omits the date at that point and inserts it at the end of the document where the parties to it put their signatures (like a cheque, the agreement *must* be dated).

The preamble usually continues by naming the parties to it. So it says, for instance: *Memorandum of Agreement made this 21st day of June 1998 between Jeremiah Bloggs of 273 Norbury Court, London SW37 9ZZ hereinafter called 'the Author' (which expression shall where the context admits include the Author's executors, administrators and assigns) and Rowes and Crowne Limited of 91 Oxford Road, London WC1X 0YY hereinafter called 'the Publisher' (which expression shall where the context admits include the Publisher's administrators, assigns or successors in business).*

Variations in this wording include 'Proprietor' instead of 'Author', which is particularly useful if the author has turned himself into a limited company, and the agreement will be between the company and the publisher, and is also perhaps more appropriate than 'Author' in cases where the rights are being signed by someone who owns the copyright but is not the author (e.g. the widow of a writer signing contracts after his death). The Publisher may be further defined, especially in these days of conglomerates, as covering any imprint in the publishing group concerned (or any future imprint of that group). You might also find additional words after the author's details such as 'of the one part' and after the publisher's details 'of the other part'. This is somewhat old-fashioned legal jargon – one doesn't hear much nowadays about 'the party of the first part and the party of the second part' – but it is not of any particular significance.

What is important is that bit about the publisher's 'assigns or successors in business', especially nowadays when the ownership of publishing houses changes with great frequency, and imprints are merged with others, or disappear totally. A great many authors worry considerably about the possibility of their publishers being taken over by someone of whom they disapprove (perhaps because of the new owner's politics, or nationality). Of course, when a publishing house is sold, the buyer expects the rights to all the books on the list to be included in the sale – there wouldn't be much point in buying the publisher without the auth.ors. But in such cases we are really talking about 'successors in business' and authors, unless they are in the bestseller category, may find it difficult to prevent the inclusion of these words. At least the passing of rights to the publisher's successors in business means that the book will still be handled by a publisher. The real danger is with 'assigns', which, in contrast, would allow the publisher to assign the rights in a book to anyone at all, publisher or not, and this is why authors increasingly often strike out any reference to assigns, and to underline the point, include such wording as Clause 23 in the MTA.

From the author's point of view there is no harm in the inclusion of 'his (i.e. the author's) executors, administrators and assigns'. An author who dies or who hands over control to an administrator (perhaps because of being no longer capable of dealing with business affairs) will expect such people to accept the agreement as binding on them, and if, for some reason the author wishes to assign the rights in the work to someone else, there is nothing to stop him from doing so (except, of course, that the publisher might want to be consulted and to be given the opportunity of opposing the assignment).

The preamble ends with some such words as 'Whereby it is mutually agreed', and it is now, as we reach the meat of the agreement, that publishers begin in earnest to show their individuality, since hardly any of them put the succeeding clauses in the same order, so that some begin by mentioning the rights which the author grants, before even recording the title of the book or giving any indication of its subject, while others start off with a clause which states that they intend to publish the book in question.

WARNING

Make sure that your name and address have been correctly inserted.

Avoid signing a document which includes 'his assigns' under the definition of 'the Publisher'. Ask for this to be deleted and for the insertion of a clause stating that the rights granted in the agreement by the author shall not be assigned without the author's consent.

THE GRANT OF RIGHTS

The main part of the agreement may start with a Grant of Rights, consisting of some such wording as *The Author grants to the Publisher the exclusive right to publish in volume form throughout the world for the duration of copyright a work entitled   written by the Author (hereinafter called 'the Work').*

Very often the wording will be more elaborate. 'Exclusive' may be expanded to 'sole and exclusive' and 'publish' to 'print, publish and sell'. 'Sole' and 'exclusive' seem to me to mean much the same, and a publisher can hardly publish unless he also prints the book (or causes it to be printed) and sells it, but lawyers often use many words when you would think that one would do, preferring precision to brevity. I suppose they are right, since a lawsuit can turn on the placing of a comma, let alone the particular words in a sentence.

(Perhaps this is the moment to deviate from the subject at hand in order to make the comment that most publishers try to make the language of their agreements as precise and legally watertight as they can. Nevertheless, the wording is not always clear, and the author should make certain that he understands it clearly. Despite all efforts at precision, some rather vague phrases are frequently to be met with – *not to be unreasonably withheld or delayed*, for instance. What exactly does 'unreasonably' mean? It can, in fact, be fairly clearly pinned down by reference to standard trade practices, the time needed for consultation, and the like, but authors and publishers may still differ in their definitions and need an arbitrator to decide between them. *Best endeavours* is another rather vague term, and a much more unsatisfactory one because one firm's 'best endeavours' may be lamentable in comparison with another's – yet who is to say that they are not 'best' for the firm concerned? Such phrases are to be avoided wherever possible, and replaced by firm commitments to a specific course of action.)

'Volume form' means that the author is granting 'volume rights', a phrase which is normally understood as the right to produce the work or license others to do so in hardcover, paperback (whether trade or mass market), and bookclub editions. Some publishers also insist that the term covers abridged or adapted versions of the book, and translation rights (i.e. the right to sell to a foreign publisher the right to publish the work in a foreign language), and even broader interpretations suggest that it can embrace all other subsidiary rights as well. If the publisher considers, as some do, that translation rights come into the subsidiary category, the clause may be varied to read '... the exclusive right to publish in volume form *in the English language* throughout the world ...', and such wording may be used for many books which British and American authors sign up with British and American publishers. Confusingly, it does not necessarily preclude the publisher from controlling translation rights, which will be covered in a later clause.

The next question to be considered is that of the territories for which the author grants the right to publish. For writers in the English language, the world is divided into at least three parts – the exclusive British market, the exclusive United States market, and the non-exclusive Open market (the rest of the world) – but there could be more divisions, with Australia and/or South Africa, for example, being removed from the exclusive British market and becoming exclusive in their own right, as it were.

(The importance of Australia as a self-contained market has, incidentally, become more significant with the introduction of the new Australian Copyright Amendment Act, which in essence gives Australian booksellers the right to import into Australia any edition of a book if it has not been made available in the country within 30 days of its first publication anywhere in the world.)

In the British market (which used to be based on the British Empire and later the British Commonwealth, but which nowadays has little such structure) only the British publisher's edition of the book may be sold; in the US market (basically the United States and its possessions) only the American publisher's edition may be sold; the same kind of arrangement will apply with an Australian or South African publisher (or any other local publisher) who has exclusive rights for the territory concerned; and in the Open Market (mainly the foreign language countries) all English language editions can be sold in competition with each other. Because the world is divided in this way as far as

English language publishing is concerned, a British publisher's contract may give him exclusive rights in the United Kingdom and in most, but not necessarily all, of the Commonwealth countries and non-exclusive rights in most foreign language countries, while the American publisher will have exclusive rights in the United States and its territories and non-exclusive rights in the foreign language countries.

A further complication has arisen because of the creation of the Common Market; the abolition of trade barriers in the EC means that American books sent for sale in Europe might infiltrate the exclusive British home market, and for this reason British publishers sometimes ask nowadays that the Continent of Europe shall be designated as part of their exclusive market (in which case it is expected that they will pay the full home royalty on their European sales, rather than the more normal export terms).

Since every book is different, the territories granted to its publisher(s) are likely to be different to a greater or a lesser degree in each case. Often the clause will define the territories with such wording as 'the exclusive right to publish the work in volume form in the territories listed in the attached Schedule'. Alternatively, as in the wording from the Grant of Rights clause quoted above, the publisher may simply ask for 'world' rights, and this will almost certainly be the case if you are selling your book to a publisher for the first time and if you do not have an agent.

There is no need to be afraid of selling world rights. If you have an agent, he will probably retain United States rights in your book (and various other rights, which will be mentioned later), and will then attempt to sell them on your behalf. On the other hand, if you do not have an agent, you might as well let the British publisher have world rights, unless you have the ability to sell US and other rights yourself, because the British publisher will try, just as an agent would, to exploit the rights on your behalf. The important thing is to make sure that the contract specifies suitable divisions of the spoils from such sales (and, again, this is a point which we shall come to later).

The next matter which requires attention in that wording quoted above is 'for the duration of copyright'. If you look at

Clause 4 of the MTA you will see that the licence given to the publisher is limited to a period of twenty years. A comparatively new concept in British publishing, this is probably the most revolutionary aspect of the MTA. It has not been universally accepted, and very many publishers still insist on a licence for the entire period of copyright, which in most cases means from publication of the book until seventy years after the author's death. You might think that to grant a licence for the duration of copyright would not necessarily be so bad a thing if the publisher were doing a good job with the book, but to limit the period of the licence does not mean that you cannot renew it with the same publisher if you are both happy to do so, nor does it prevent you from reverting your rights at an earlier date if you have due cause. What it does allow you to do is to move to another publisher if you so desire, or to renegotiate the terms of the agreement with your existing publisher, at the end of the licence period.

Renegotiation could be of particular benefit to an author whose first book has been extremely successful – since he was a first-time author when the book was signed up, the terms of the contract might not have been as generous as those for an established bestseller, but renegotiation can put this right. It is largely for this reason that the MTA suggests (Clause 4b) that before the expiry of the licence period (indeed, half-way through in the example shown), either party to the contract can ask for the terms to be revised.

If the licence is to be a limited one, either at this point in the agreement or later, there will be a clause laying down the conditions under which the licence may be renewed. The MTA insists (Clause 4c) that the work shall be in print, but let us suppose that the book has gone out of print because of lack of demand, the author has not bothered to revert the rights, and then the news has come that the book is to be turned into a television serial – in such circumstances renewal might take place despite the book being out of print. Note that the wording of the MTA (Clause 4c) allows the author to bring into the negotiations for renewal any offer for the book that he may have received from another publisher, and that it clarifies the position of any existing sub-licences.

However desirable a limited-period licence may be, few publishers are willing to contract for books on this basis, and your agreement is more likely to specify that the publisher will retain the right to publish for the whole period of copyright. There is no need to worry unduly on this score, so long as the circumstances in which rights may revert are satisfactory and clearly set out (see pp. 122-6).

Note that whether the licence period is limited or is for the full term of copyright, the author's copyright itself is not surrendered. Indeed, there should be a later clause which specifically states that the author's copyright will be acknowledged in all copies of the book. The term 'copyright' is another word for ownership; as soon as you have written something original, whether recorded on paper or on a computer disc, or recorded in some other way, the copyright in it is yours – the ownership of the material is immediately vested in you. Licensing a publisher to publish your work does not diminish your copyright in it. If someone copies it, or a part of it, without permission, or if a publisher produces copies of it without having been given a licence, then your copyright is infringed. You can sell your copyright if you wish, though it is rarely a course to be recommended.

Most publishers do not ask to purchase the author's copyright, but a few unscrupulous companies do, and the practice is not unknown among highly-respected academic houses, although in most cases they use standard royalty contracts.

The rogue publishers' aim is simply to increase their profits on books which they expect to have a long life, probably in several formats. The outright sum offered may sound very generous, but will be a very small proportion of the amount that the author would receive if royalties were paid. Moreover, the publisher would be free to mutilate the text in any way he wanted, and the author's name might not appear on any editions. An impecunious author may find it difficult to turn down an outright offer, especially when the publisher says, 'If you won't take it, I can easily find others who will.' But it is worth remembering that if the rogue publisher believes in the success of the book, others who do not cheat their authors are also likely to be interested in it, so the work may find a better home elsewhere.

The academic houses are rather different, and have some justification in claiming that it is trade practice for outright purchase of copyright in some of the monographs they publish. This is because certain dons who want to see their theses in print are not so much interested in financial rewards, as in the prestige which publication will bring.

It is said that authors who relinquish their copyright not only harm themselves but let down all other authors. But this pronouncement has the weakness of all generalizations, and there are exceptional cases in which the usual arguments for retention of copyright must be set aside.

Authors are usually required to give up their copyright in work for inclusion in encyclopaedias, which may have several hundred contributors, or for a yearbook containing essays by a number of different writers. It is normal practice to do so, for a number of reasons: it would clearly be impractical to pay a royalty to all contributors to such publications, consultation on sub-licences, jackets and other matters would be impossible, and the publishers would not be able to take swift action, which depends on the approval of the copyright owners, against the piracy of their books if they had first to seek clearance from hundreds of contributors. There is, however, a solution which some publishers adopt, paying an initial fee to cover the first printing, and further fees each time the book is reprinted.

A partial exception to the rule of never parting with your copyright may be made in the case of the packaged book. Packagers put together highly illustrated books, using many pages in colour, which they sell in completed book form in different languages across the world (if they can) to regular publishers, thus building up a very large print quantity, and reducing the costs of the colour printing. The packager is responsible for everything up to stocking, publicizing and selling the book, which is the publisher's job. The text is usually written to order by an author commissioned by the packager, who may sometimes wish to buy the copyright, paying a substantial fee, arguing that since he originated the idea, he has some claim to ownership of the text, which in any case he needs in order to have total control of the book. There is some justice in his argument, but not a lot. The author should not give up his copyright, and should ask instead that his fee should be payable in the form of a royalty on the price received by the packager, or that the fee should be related to the quantity of the book printed, with additional fees being paid for increases in that quantity or for reprints. The packager would still have control of the text, and the right to publish it or license others to do so for the licence period laid down in the agreement.

Reverting to the Grant of Rights quoted above, the last part of the wording refers to 'a work entitled ....' What is put in the blank space may be simply the agreed title of a completed book, or a tentative or working title, or something far more complex, referring to a synopsis and/or specimen chapters, to correspondence between the publisher and the author, and of course it may also contain details to clarify whether 'the author' is in fact an author, or an editor, a compiler, or whatever may be appropriate. There may also be a statement of the expected length of the work, and specifications relating to illustrations, index, the responsibility for obtaining permission to use any material the copyright of which belongs to others, etc. It is a good idea to include all relevant detail, so that both parties know what is expected. Some publishers, as well as laying down their requirements in precise terms, ask for progress reports from their authors, and even if the prime intention is simply to assure themselves that the book is likely to be delivered on time, it seems to me a sensible idea to have fixed dates at which the author can not only tell the publisher what progress he has made and of any problems he has encountered, but can report in sufficient detail for the publisher to see exactly what sort of book he will be getting and to be able to steer the author back on to the rails if he thinks he has gone off them. If that kind of procedure were followed more often, there would be fewer cases of commissioned books being rejected on delivery because they were not what the publisher expected and wanted.

WARNING
Make sure that you understand what rights you are selling. Don't get confused with FBSR – First British Serial Rights – or any other serial rights, which are what you sell to a magazine or newspaper.

If the contract gives the publisher the right to publish abridged or adapted versions or 'any substantial part' of the work, ensure that your written consent is necessary before he can do so.

Check carefully to see what territories you are granting to your publisher and make sure that you are entitled to grant them. Seek expert advice (see Chapter 14). If you have no agent, don't be afraid to give the publisher world rights (but make sure, of course, that you receive adequate percentages of the income from US and translation sales, and especially with regard to subsidiary rights granted to foreign publishers (see p.113).

Try to persuade your publisher to accept a limited licence period, or at least to allow you to renegotiate terms if the book is still in print after, say, ten years. If you fail, don't worry too much – it is not yet standard practice. But ask him again with your next book, and go on asking, because the world is changing and even the old diehards have to move with the times.

Never give up your copyright. What, never? Well, hardly ever. If you are offered an outright payment which will mean surrendering your copyright, ask the publisher why he is putting forward a deal of this sort. If the answer is that the material is to be part of an encyclopaedia or yearbook, or if there is some other genuine reason which makes a royalty agreement impractical, you should probably accept the situation. However, you should ask for further payments each time the book is reprinted. If the publisher cannot justify the outright offer (and uses the argument that if you don't accept, there are many others who will), at least get as much money out of him as you can.

The author must check that all details concerning the contents and material for the book are correct, and that he and the publisher are talking about exactly the same project. If the details are not clear in the agreement, the various points should be clarified in an exchange of correspondence (make sure that you keep the letters from the publisher and copies of your own letters) and this correspondence should be attached to the contract.

SUBSIDIARY RIGHTS
Although subsidiary or secondary rights are most often

covered in a clause or clauses later in the agreement, it seems reasonable to define them at this stage (the split of income from them will be considered later), since when they are spelt out in an agreement they are in fact expanding on or qualifying the Grant of Rights.

Considerable confusion exists over which rights should be included under the heading 'Subsidiary Rights'. Some publishers regard any or all of paperback, bookclub, translation and United States (or Canadian, Australian, or any other English language) rights as being covered by 'volume rights', and if, for instance, world English language volume rights are granted to the publisher in the Preamble, any or all of those specific rights may not be mentioned in a Subsidiary Rights clause. Moreover, in that part of the contract which deals with the split of moneys between the publisher and the author, these rights will probably be given separate clauses, instead of being lumped in with other subsidiary rights. It really does not matter a great deal what the rights are called, provided that the agreement makes clear at some point or other exactly which rights the author has licensed the publisher to handle.

If you have an agent, he will usually wish to remove from the publisher the right to handle US, first serial, dramatic, film, radio and television, translation and merchandizing rights, and he may also want to control paperback and second serial rights as well, himself selling, or attempting to sell, all these rights on your behalf. This will leave the publisher with little more than bookclub, and anthology and quotation rights. If you do not have an agent, it will very probably be worth your while to allow the publisher to look after all these rights, since he will have someone on his staff whose job it is to try to sell them, and who will try actively to do so, since the publisher will then receive a share of the proceeds.

A Subsidiary Rights list will almost certainly include:

First Serial Rights. These refer to the appearance of the book or part of the book in a magazine or newspaper *prior to* its publication in book form. So 'first' in this context simply means 'before publication of the book'. Confusingly, the term 'serial' does not necessarily mean that the book will be reproduced in a number of parts in a series of issues of the magazine or newspaper. In this context 'serial' is a bit of publishing jargon, and is really another name for a magazine or newspaper. So there can be one extract or a whole series of extracts.

Second Serial Rights. These refer to the appearance of the book or part of it in a magazine or newspaper *after* its publication in book form. To continue the confusion, the term 'second serial' is used whether the serialization is the first, second or umpteenth after book publication – they are all 'second'. So 'second' simply means 'after publication of the book'.

Anthology and Quotation Rights. If someone wants to reproduce part of your work in an anthology, he should seek permission from the publisher, who will charge a fee for the use of your work. The same thing applies if someone wants to quote a passage from your work within his own text (although a fee may not be charged if it is merely a short extract, by which is usually meant not more than 400 words – see Chapter 12). Similarly, if you yourself want to use copyright material, the publisher of the book from which you want to take an extract will be able to deal with your request under the Anthology Rights clause in his contract with the author concerned.

Digest Rights and Digest Book Condensation Rights. These differ from each other according to whether, in the former case, the abridged form of the work is to appear in a magazine or newspaper, or, in the latter case, in book form. Some publishers use 'Abridgement Rights' to mean the shortened work appearing in book form, and you may notice that in the MTA (Clause 18a iii) the distinction is made clear by reference to 'Condensation rights – magazines' and 'Condensation rights – books'.

One-shot periodical Rights. This refers to the publication of a book in its entirety in a single issue of a newspaper or magazine.

Hardcover Reprint, Loose Leaf, and Large Print Rights. Hardcover reprint rights are most likely to apply if your book is the kind which another publisher might wish to include in a series – a 'Library of Travellers' Tales', for instance, or 'Classics of World War II'. Loose leaf publication refers to the comparatively rare format known as Filofiction, in which a novel is produced as unbound sheets with punchings to suit Filofax binders. Large print setting is widely used, especially for fiction, in producing books for the partially sighted; the author gains doubly, because the books are popular in public libraries and Public Lending Right moneys can be earned on them.

Strip Cartoon Rights. These are becoming increasingly important, with the publication of many successful novels in strip cartoon form.

Merchandizing Rights. These can include all manner of things – diaries, notebooks and many artefacts far removed from paper and print, ranging from mugs to T-shirts and far beyond. In some cases, a purchaser of film rights will insist that the deal cannot be completed unless merchandizing rights are available and included in the package which he is buying.

Dramatic Rights. These usually cover stage, radio and television.

Film Rights. Purchasers of film rights may also require permission to use up to 7,500 words, extracted from the book, or summarized from it, for publicity purposes, and some publishers insert a clause giving them the right to grant such permission.

Radio and Television Reading Rights. This term covers only straight readings from the work, not dramatized versions. Not all publishers include the word 'Reading' and it is worth getting it put in. Even better is a definition, perhaps added in brackets, such as 'the right to give single-voice readings'.

Microphotographic Reproduction Rights. Usually restricted to the complete work only.

Sound and Video Recording Rights. The rights to make audio cassettes from published books have become increasingly important in recent years, and some publishers now have a division specifically devoted to their production. It is worth noting that sound recording rights may also appear in a clause concerned with Braille editions of the work (see p.63).

Reprographic Rights. Photocopiers are to be found everywhere, and many of their users appear to think that they are entitled to make photocopies of anything they like, including copyright work. They are in fact allowed to make copies of a limited amount of material for their own private use, but it is illegal to make a copy or copies of a complete book or to make several copies of an extract, as teachers have sometimes done for each pupil in a class, or as some industrial concerns and others do for members of their staffs. It is, alas, impossible to stop people from photocopying copyright material, and the only alternative was to set up the Copyright Licensing Agency, which issues licences to allow photocopying under certain conditions and with the payment of fees. The CLA is jointly owned by the Publishers Licensing Society (PLS) and the Authors' Licensing and Collecting Society (ALCS), and fees collected are split between them. In the case of books it is usual for 50% to go to the author and 50% to the publisher, but this split does not necessarily apply to material photocopied from magazines and journals, especially academic publications, in which the publisher may own all the relevant rights. When the author takes a share it is distributed to him by the ALCS. All publishers' agreements should include a clause which states that reprographic rights shall be granted by the publisher to PLS and by the author to ALCS. Sometimes the clause will also make it clear that this does not refer to the actual typography of the work, which belongs to the publisher, and which he may licence another publisher to use.

Electronic Rights. The ownership of these rights, which cover CD-Roms, Internet publishing, e-books, and any other means of reproducing books electronically, including those as yet unknown, is a subject on which publishers hold diametrically opposed views to those of authors and agents. Publishers claim that the rights are part of volume rights, and should therefore be in their control, a position which the others dispute. The two sides are also divided when it comes to agreeing on the split between them of any income earned by the sale of electronic rights. See also pp. 178–9.

Other Rights. An additional sub-clause should make it clear that Public Lending Right and any other rights not specifically mentioned or described, including any which may be developed in the future, shall remain the author's property. So if your contract does not include any mention of electronic (or any other) rights, do not despair, because you will be covered by this sub-clause. You will probably also be covered even without it, because if any right arises which is not specifically mentioned in the contract, the author and the publisher can usually jointly agree on how it will be handled and on the appropriate split of any moneys concerned. Technicological advances mean that new rights are constantly coming into being.

Public Lending Right *always* belongs to the author, and that fact is enshrined in the Act which brought PLR into being. Any money that you earn through PLR is paid to you direct, so that you do not have to share it with anyone and even if you have an agent it is one form of income from a book which he has sold for you on which you pay no commission. It is, however, the author's responsibility to obtain, fill in and despatch PLR forms and himself to solve any connected problems. It is not the publisher's job, nor the agent's to undertake any of these tasks, and neither of them should be asked to do so. In any case, it is not difficult to apply for PLR, and the people who administrate the scheme are both efficient and extremely helpful.

As already explained, if the following rights are not the subject of separate clauses, the Subsidiary Rights Clause may also include:

Paperback Rights. These may cover all paperback editions, whether they are mass market or 'trade paperbacks' (usually rather better produced and rather more highly priced than the common-or-garden mass market version) and whether they are published by the publisher whose agreement this is, or are licensed to an outside publishing house. It is perhaps worth pointing out that when, shortly after World War II, the paperback 'revolution' really took off and mass market paperbacks began to replace the hardcover publisher's cheap editions, paperbacks were produced almost exclusively by specialist publishers who were independent of the hardcover houses. The hardcover publishers were always the first publishers of the books, and the paperback companies purchased from them the right (on a licence for a limited period) to produce a paperback edition, usually after a fairly long delay. That way of working still survives, but recent years have seen a substantial growth in what is known as 'vertical' publishing, with the hardcover publisher owning his own mass market paperback company (or vice versa), and buying books with the purpose of producing both hard and soft cover editions, which sometimes appear simultaneously. Paperback rights are frequently considered as coming under the heading 'Subsidiary Rights' only when they are licensed to a different concern, belonging among volume rights when published by the house which has drawn up the original agreement.

Bookclub Rights. These cover both copies of the publisher's own editions of the book which he sells to the bookclub, and editions produced by the bookclub itself.

United States Rights. If a British publisher succeeds in selling US rights (and the same applies to the relevant rights in other English-speaking countries such as Canada, Australia and South Africa), he may sign an agreement very similar to his own, granting the US publisher exactly the same sort of rights for the US territories as he himself controls in the British territories, with the payment of an advance, and royalties and the sharing of income from subsidiary rights. In this case, the US publisher will usually be responsible for the manufacture of his own editions. Alternatively, the British publisher may wish to sell the US publisher bound copies or sheets (i.e. the printed pages, unbound) of his own edition, normally identical with it, except for the US publisher's imprint on the titlepage (and also on the jacket and binding, and with a dollar price, if he is supplying bound copies). These copies may be sold to the US publisher either on a royalty inclusive basis (in which case the author will receive his percentage on the total shipment), or with the US publisher paying royalties on his sales of the book (when the author may receive more per copy, but only of course in accordance with the actual sales).

Translation Rights. These are sometimes called 'Foreign Rights', a term which can cause confusion for unenlightened authors who may think that it covers the sale of the English language edition of the work in foreign countries. It does not. Such sales come under 'Export Sales'. Translation Rights, if granted to the publisher, give him the right to negotiate with a foreign language publisher and to sell him, for instance, German language rights, or Finnish or

Japanese language rights. These will usually be world rights in the language concerned (except sometimes in the case of Spanish and Portuguese, since there are different publishing industries in these languages in Europe and in South America), and will allow the foreign language publisher to handle the sale and licensing of paperback, bookclub and other subsidiary rights in his own language. He will also be responsible for choosing and paying a translator.

Braille editions. Some agreements will include a special clause giving the publisher the right to authorize transcription of the work into Braille. Traditionally, permission is given without payment to either the publisher or the author, but with a requirement that due acknowledgement to the title, the author and the publisher is made and that the copyright notice is included. Similar concessions are made for Talking Books and other recordings for the blind (which may be mentioned in the same clause), but care is needed since readings of books on tape are often available for sale to the public at large, and are rapidly increasing in popularity; if they are not specifically provided free of charge for the blind, there is no reason why the author should not receive a royalty on the sales of such recordings.

WARNING

Be sure that you there is nothing to stop you from granting the rights specified in the agreement.

Be careful to ensure that there is a clause covering any rights not specifically mentioned and that it leaves such rights in your control, not the publisher's, even though you may wish, when the question arises, to allow him to handle the rights with an appropriate share of any resulting income.

Make sure that the publisher is not attempting to take any part of your public lending rights. One or two publishers still try to pretend that they are entitled to a share in PLR, but there are *no* circumstances in which they are entitled to do so (and that is true even if you have asked the publisher to make application to the PLR administrators in respect of your work – which you should not have done anyway).

Take care to see that all subsidiary rights are listed – especially paperback, bookclub, US and translation rights. Some publishers have a blanket clause which refers to sub-leasing or sub-licensing of rights without specifying what the rights may be, and this may result in the author receiving far less than a fair share of the moneys involved.

II   THE AUTHOR'S OBLIGATIONS

DELIVERY OF THE TYPESCRIPT

The first clause dealing with the author's obligations is likely to be one which specifies the date by which the typescript or disc is to be delivered. The date should be agreed between the author and the publisher before the contract is drawn up, and should be a realistic one from the author's point of view. While publishers are usually fairly tolerant of an author's delay in delivering a typescript, there is no point in inserting a totally unrealistic date. If the publisher, for some reason such as the topical nature of the book, simply must have the material in his hands on a given date, this should be agreed beforehand, and the author who is late in such circumstances can hardly be surprised if the agreement is cancelled. If there is no particular urgency, provided that delivery is not absurdly overdue, and especially if there is some good reason for the delay, most publishers are prepared to ignore any wording which threatens that if the author is late in delivery he will be given a very short time in which to make good his shortcoming, and if he fails to do so the contract will be cancelled, and he will have to return his advance. Truly professional authors pride themselves on their ability to keep to delivery dates and, if they foresee that they will be late, are careful to give their publishers advance warning. However, we are all subject to illness from time to time, and the contract should specify some let-out for the author if he is unable to deliver the typescript on time for this reason, or indeed because of other circumstances beyond his control.

Most publishers' contracts nowadays will require the author to deliver hard copy (i.e. a typescript) and a disc containing the text in a word-processing format which is compatible with that used by the publisher and the printer. (Do not despair if you do not have a computer – typescripts are still acceptable – but think about getting one, because discs will soon become mandatory; alternatively, employ a secretarial service agency to prepare a disc from your typescript.) The disc (or if you have supplied two typescripts, one of them) will go to the printer. The hard copy will be used for a number of purposes within the publishing house, including the preparation of the jacket. Some publishers insert an instruction in their agreements which compels the author to have and to keep an additional copy of the typescript or of the material on disc for his own use; of course, all wise authors do keep their own copy – it's a sensible precaution against any loss or damage which may occur (and many publishers, incidentally, include a clause freeing them from any responsibility for loss or damage while the author's material is in their possession, although this should always be qualified by wording such as 'except in the case of loss or damage as a result of negligence on the part of the publisher or his employees').

The contract may also make mention of the standard of the work on delivery. The MTA speaks of a work which is 'professionally competent' and some agents have a clause which refers to a 'satisfactory' typescript, but publishers' agreements will usually demand that the typescript shall be complete, in some cases that it shall be 'ready for press', and very often that it shall be acceptable to the publisher. Later in this chapter the question of the publisher's acceptance of the typescript will be dealt with in some detail, but at this stage I am concerned only with the wording 'complete' and 'ready for press'. The fact that the publisher wants the completed work by the due date is hardly surprising or in any way exceptionable, but the author must realize that this means not only the text in a fully revised condition (rather than at draft stage), but also all additional material, such as notes, appendices, illustrations, etc, which the author is due to supply. (If the author is to prepare the index, this cannot be done until proof stage, but the publisher will want to know before the book goes to the printer what the index length is likely to be.) 'Ready for press' is a phrase which requires some definition, and it is fairly important that the author should discover exactly what the publisher means by it. He may mean simply that the typescript should be legible (no pale grey typewriter or word processor ribbons), reasonably clean (not too many alterations), and not requiring a considerable amount of correction of spelling, punctuation, grammar, etc. Not that publishers expect perfection, and only rarely does a book go from delivery straight to the printer without further work being done on it – the editor may suggest changes to the text, which could even involve a major rewrite, and the copy editor may point out all manner of necessary amendments (not only of a grammatical nature, but also concerned with errors of fact, inconsistencies, etc). On the other hand, publishers nowadays frequently do not employ copy editors, and may therefore interpret 'ready for press' to mean that the author has undertaken his own copy-editing – a skilled job which very few writers could carry out competently.

WARNING

Don't agree to a delivery date which you know or fear you won't be able to adhere to. If you find at a later stage that you are going to be late, let the publisher know.

Clarify the meaning of 'ready for press' if those words appear in the delivery clause.

ILLUSTRATIONS AND OTHER COPYRIGHT MATERIAL

If the book is to contain illustrations, the contract will probably include a reference to them, often specifying the quantity and nature of the illustrative material. If the copyright in question belongs to someone other than the author, either the agreement or an accompanying letter should spell out whose responsibility it will be to obtain and pay for the necessary permissions.

If the book includes extensive quotations from copyright work, or if it uses in any way other material, such as tables and graphs, which is copyright, it is quite likely that no specific mention of responsibility for obtaining and paying for the necessary permissions will be included in the contract, because the publisher will rely on the Warranty clause (see p. 71) in which the author guarantees that the work does not infringe anyone else's copyright, and therefore implies that, if copyright material has been included, clearance has been given.

Whether dealing with illustrations or with copyright material of any other kind, normal practice is indeed for the author to obtain the necessary permissions, although the publisher's advice should be sought first, to discover, for instance, whether permission is required for use throughout the world, or perhaps only in the British market. The MTA states very firmly (Clause 3a) that the publisher should be responsible for all the fees, or at the very least should contribute a sum of up to £250 towards them. Many publishers will baulk at this, insisting that such payment shall be entirely the author's responsibility, but in such cases it is certainly worth trying to negotiate a compromise.

WARNING

Don't think you can get away with not clearing permissions, or believe that your publisher will automatically deal with the matter without being asked to do so. Indeed the majority of publishers will express very strongly the view that the clearance of permissions and the fees for them should be exclusively the author's concern. They argue that they are paying the author for the whole book, and if there's any part of it that he doesn't himself write, then it's up to him to pay for whoever's copyright work it may be.

Make sure that if there is to be any sharing of the responsibilities for obtaining permissions, both you and the publisher know exactly what each of you will undertake, and who will pay any bills, and if the publisher is prepared to shoulder some of the cost, how much he will pay.

Before clearing permissions, ask your publisher what rights and territories you should ask for. If you can afford it, always clear world rights – it will avoid problems if the book is sold, for instance, to a United States publisher or, indeed, anywhere abroad, and may also be cheaper in the long run.

You do not actually need to clear and pay for the permissions until the book is complete, and has been delivered to the publisher, and when you are sure that he intends to go ahead. However, it is certainly worth while to check beforehand on what the charges are likely to be for any material you want to use. The costs can be enormous, especially if you are quoting from 'big name' authors or are perhaps intending to reproduce artwork by a famous painter whose work is in copyright (don't rely on the fact that the artist has been dead for a very long time – institutions such as the National Portrait Gallery charge quite heavy reproduction fees for canvases which they own, even if the painter went to the Great Studio in the Sky several centuries ago). Beware in particular of quoting from the lyrics of pop songs – you might say that the fees demanded are beyond the dreams of avarice, were it not clear that avarice is wide awake, and has no time for anything as fanciful as dreams.

Beware of the apparently kindly publisher who suggests that he will help you to meet the cost of clearing permissions by increasing the amount of the advance which he originally offered. Unless the original advance was extremely unlikely to be earned, all that he is doing is offering you a loan out of the eventual royalties on the book – in other words, he is lending you your own money. Any sum paid by the publisher for the clearance of permissions should be entirely separate from the advance and from royalties. Of course, if you have undertaken to pay all the permission fees, and you need a loan from the publisher, which he is willing to provide, in order to meet them, that's OK, as long as you both recognize that it is a loan, and not a generous increase in the advance.

INDEX

The publisher may also require the author to supply, at his own expense, an index for the book. However, the preparation of an index is a highly skilled job, especially if the book is long and complex, and the author may be unwilling to undertake the task. It is also possible that, even if the author is willing, the publisher will doubt his ability to do the job competently. In either of those cases, the publisher will engage a professional indexer, and the MTA states (Clause 3b) that the cost will be divided equally between author and publisher, the author's share being deducted from moneys due to him under later clauses in the contract. Publishers who are not signatories of the MTA may wish to send the author a bill, expecting immediate cash settlement, arguing, with some justification, that if the author's advance remains unearned, as is the case more frequently than either party would wish, they will end up paying the bill themselves. It is important to make sure that the responsibilities and the financial arrangements are clearly delineated, especially since professional indexers do not come cheap.

WARNING

Don't take on the job of preparing the Index if you are not capable of doing it adequately.

Beware of the apparently kindly publisher who suggests that he will help you to meet the cost of the index by increasing the amount of the advance which he originally offered. The same comments apply as those already made in the section above in respect of permissions.

REVISED EDITIONS

Most non-fiction contracts carry a clause requiring the author to update or otherwise revise the book from time to time, or, if he is unwilling or unable to do so, to allow the publisher to arrange for someone else to undertake the work. Although no definition of the amount of alteration is given, the intention of the clause is clearly not simply to cover a few minor changes, but envisages that the new version of the book will be substantially different from its predecessor. If the publisher has to employ someone other than the author to do the necessary work, the publisher is usually entitled to deduct the cost from payments due to the author. The MTA (Clause 22) suggests that 'if reasonable', whatever that may mean, an additional advance should be paid to the author by the publisher when the former undertakes such a revision, and some of its signatories have even made such payments standard, leaving out the undefined 'if reasonable' proviso. Most publishers, however, will probably expect authors to undertake revision of their work without extra pay, arguing that the sales of the revised edition should be compensation enough.

Some agreements carry a proviso in this clause that if the revised edition entails resetting the entire book, the royalties, if they have reached a higher level on the original edition, shall revert to their starting point. This would seem to be a matter which should be discussed and settled in accordance with the circumstances, rather than regarded as cut-and-dried.

WARNING

Any decision concerning the need for a revised edition should be taken jointly by the publisher and the author, but authors should realize that publishers will often need convincing that the revision is really necessary.

If the author is unwilling for some reason to undertake the revision, it is important that he should ascertain exactly what charge the publisher will be making against his royalties, and argue if the fee seems unnecessarily high.

WARRANTY

Not all publishers would include the warranty under the author's obligations, but it seems to me very reasonable to deal with it here. A warranty is a legal term with much the same meaning as 'guarantee' – it is a statement which the person making it warrants or guarantees to be true. In publishers' contracts the author's warranty usually covers several matters.

Firstly, the author must declare that the work is original, that he is its owner and has the right to sign a contract in respect of it, and that it has not been published elsewhere previously. Cynics might say that nothing can possibly be original, but in the context in which the word is used it really means that the author originated or created the work, rather than that it is totally different from anything ever published before, and it is perhaps to make this clear that the wording 'original to him (the author)' is sometimes used. For an author to warrant that the work is original is also to guarantee that he has not been guilty of plagiarism (i.e. copying another author's work), and that permission has been or will be obtained to quote or use in any way material which is someone else's copyright, but this matter is more properly covered in a later part of the clause. Being the owner of the work and free to sign a contract in respect of it hardly requires clarification, except perhaps to say to the naive that if you have once signed a contract in respect of your work you mustn't sign another contract for the same book and covering the same rights unless the first contract has been cancelled. Finally, the point that the book has not been published elsewhere previously usually means in volume form and does not preclude you from signing the contract if, for instance, the work has previously been published in the USA (provided of course that you did not give the American publisher any rights of which he could make use in the exclusive territories which you are now granting to the British publisher). However, it would be only courteous to tell the publisher with whom you are now signing a contract of any earlier publication of the work in whatever form and wherever it took place. Clearly, if you were signing a contract in respect of a book now to be reissued, it would be essential to strike out these words.

Secondly, the author will be called upon to warrant that the work does not infringe anyone else's copyright or other rights, nor contain any libellous, obscene or otherwise unlawful material. The first of these requirements covers the matter of plagiarism and permissions to use copyright material mentioned briefly above – it is both immoral and illegal to copy someone else's work, a point which may perhaps be even clearer if plagiarism is factually defined quite simply as 'stealing'. Please note, this applies even if the book from which the material comes has been long out of print and even if the publishers who originally issued it are no longer in existence. As for infringing other rights of other persons, it might involve a possible invasion of privacy, and alternatively you have only to think of such buzz words as racism and sexism to understand what could also be meant here. On the other hand, you may not be so familiar with 'moral rights' (see p. 95), which, when they belong to someone else, are also protected under this clause. Libellous material is certainly to be avoided – to be sued for libel can be unpleasant, very time-consuming and extremely expensive (for a discussion of the subject, see my book, *An Author's Guide to Publishing*). As for 'obscene', you may feel that absolutely anything goes nowadays, but this is not really true – there are still certain areas, such as the sexual abuse of children, which the general public and perhaps the Director of Public Prosecutions may still find offensive in the extreme (and pro-censorship moral watchdogs can make trouble over far less contentious matters than that). What else could be covered by 'otherwise unlawful'? Since we do not live in a police state we are free to publish anti-monarchical material, for instance, without being accused of treason; we can attack the police; and although racism and sexism may be anathema, we can publish comments which people of non-Christian creeds find violently offensive without offending against the laws of this country (although we may, like Salman Rushdie, find that we are in serious trouble with foreign zealots); however, there are many matters which would come under the heading 'otherwise unlawful', and these include anything which is covered by the Official Secrets Act (that extremely boring book, *Spycatcher*, was swept to bestsellerdom by the British Government's claim that it infringed the Act and was therefore unlawful), and there are still laws in place which protect the Christian religion against blasphemy (even if it would have to be pretty extreme nowadays to result in prosecution).

Next, the clause will probably demand that the author should warrant that the statements purporting to be facts in the book are true and that no instructions in it, if followed with reasonable care, would cause injury to the reader or anyone else. The second part of this warranty is immediately understandable and a matter of common sense (although my agent points out that the wording should be removed in the case of a whodunit or thriller, since, he says, 'one hopes that the formula for a good murder *would* be injurious if followed with reasonable care!'). However, the first part of this section of the warranty seems to me to ask rather a lot. I am not sure whether it is really possible always to separate something which may merely be an author's opinion on some matter from 'a statement purporting to be a fact'; however, this part of the clause is usually taken, I believe, to refer only to matters which are likely to prove controversial, and even then there is a fair amount of latitude. Whatever the interpretation, it is very desirable (and this is a point in which the MTA quoted in this book might be considered faulty) that the wording should be 'the statements purporting to be facts in the book are true *to the best of the author's knowledge and belief*' (even if the publisher later wanted some reassurance that the author had actually checked his facts).

Having said that, it is important to understand that the whole warranty or any part of it can be overridden by agreement between the author and the publisher. Even at the stage of a commission, and certainly if the book has already been written, the publisher may be well aware that it is libellous or obscene or that it offends against the Official

Secrets Act, but may be perfectly willing to go ahead with it nonetheless. In such cases, it is essential that the matter should be discussed openly between the author and the publisher, and correspondence should record the fact that the publisher accepts full liability for his acceptance of and willingness to publish the unlawful material. In contrast, many publishers include a provision allowing them to refuse to continue with the planned publication if they become aware of unlawful material in the book and if the author refuses to amend it.

The next section of the clause contains the penalties which the author will incur if he gives a warranty which proves to be untrue – if, despite his promise to the contrary, the work does indeed infringe someone else's copyright, or is libellous, or injurious or 'otherwise unlawful'. In such cases the author, the publisher and the printer will probably be sued or prosecuted, and the action may extend to sub-licensees, such as bookclubs and paperback publishers. The author will be required to indemnify the publisher against his costs and losses, which could amount to a huge sum of money, especially as he will also be responsible for seeing that the printer is not out of pocket, and may have to indemnify those sub-licensees too. Even if the case against the book is dropped before it gets to court and even if no settlement is made, the publisher is likely to have a hefty bill in lawyer's fees, and he'll be entitled to pass it on to the author. Don't think, by the way, that your nice friendly publisher, who is after all only a cog in the vast and extremely wealthy machine of which his imprint is a tiny part – don't think that he will say, 'That's all right, my friend – our huge conglomerate will stand the cost and the loss.' Don't even believe that he won't ask you to cough up because he knows that all authors are penniless and it will be a waste of his time to try to extract any money from you. He will do his best to reduce his losses by getting anything from you that he can, and he will rightly be quite ruthless in doing so, if you have deliberately given a false warranty. On the other hand, if you have been honest with your publisher throughout, and then find that you have inadvertently offended, he is likely to be entirely supportive of you and as generous as is possible for him. Nevertheless, even in such cases the costs may be staggeringly high.

Most publishers go on to attach to the warranty clause a paragraph stating that they shall have the right to choose which solicitors or counsel they shall use in defence of any actions against the book, and that the author shall co-operate with them in the defence.

Publishers invariably expect the author's warranty to survive the termination of the contract, which means that although the book is out of print and the agreement has been cancelled and the rights have reverted to the author, if a libel case, for instance, is brought against the publisher in respect of the book, he will still be able to rely on the author's warranty and the obligations it places upon him.

WARNING

Take the warranty very seriously, and if you have the slightest hesitation, don't sign it without discussing the matter openly with your publisher.

If you have been commissioned to write the book, let your publisher know when you deliver it if anything in it has changed from the way it was envisaged and is now likely to conflict with your acceptance of the clause when you signed the contract.

Unaccountably, the MTA quoted in this book contains a provision that the author shall indemnify the publisher against any claim *alleging* breach of his warranty. Although the clause goes on to exclude claims which the publisher deems to be groundless, vexatious or purely malicious, this really isn't good enough from the author's point of view, especially since the decision for or against exclusion is left entirely to the publisher. If the warranty is breached, the author is clearly guilty; if the breach is merely alleged and not proven, he is innocent, and should not suffer. Is it unreasonable to suggest that in the latter case any costs should be borne by the publisher as a matter of normal business? At the very least, if this wording appears in your contract you should raise the matter with the publisher and see if you can get it deleted. It might be that the publisher is extremely reluctant to make any change because he carries insurance against libel and the terms of the insurance insist that the exact wording of his warranty clause should be retained; in that case, the author should find out whether the insurance covers him as well as the publisher, and if so on what terms.

PROOFS

Virtually all publishers include a clause in their agreements which says that the author will correct the proofs of the work. It is a job which most authors do willingly, if not always skilfully (it isn't easy), and it is to be hoped that nowadays no author will get a nasty shock in finding, at proof stage, that his book has been altered by the publisher without either permission from the author or having had the courtesy to let him know of the changes. It is an indictment of many publishers' attitude toward authors that nasty shocks of this kind still happen all too frequently.

Most agreements give the author two weeks in which to correct the proofs – the MTA (Clause 7b) specifies 15 working days, which is close on three weeks – but some publishers ask for them back more quickly than that, and go on with nasty remarks about the publisher being allowed to get someone else to read the proofs if the author doesn't return them in time – and guess who pays for that. An equally unpleasant alternative is that if the author doesn't send them back on the due date, the publisher will consider them as passed for press, which presumably does not mean that he will let the book go through unread and possibly full of printer's errors, but that he will not give the author any other opportunity of reading the proofs and incorporating any amendments to the text, nor will he listen to any later complaints from him about essential alterations left unchanged.

One of the most important points in any clause about proofs is the provision that if the author's corrections exceed a given percentage of the cost of composition of the whole book (i.e. setting the book up in print), the author will pay any excess charges. Most publishers fix the figure at 10%, but the MTA gives a more generous 15%. Whichever figure is given, don't be misled into thinking that if you alter 10% (or 15%) of the book in the proofs you won't have to pay – the cost of each minor correction is extremely high, and comparatively few alterations will soon take you over the limit. This is why, if instead of using the percentage basis your publisher gives an actual figure, saying for example that you will have to pay if the cost of your corrections exceeds £10, you will have to be very careful indeed – £10 does not give you much scope. The answer is to make every effort to ensure that the typescript which goes to the printer is free of errors. If the book is illustrated, the cost of making alterations to the pictures will include the origination of the artwork, so again you need to be very careful to make sure that everything is right before it goes to the printer and then to keep any alterations to the absolute minimum. I must applaud those rare publishers who promise that if the author's corrections are going to be costly they will let him know and give him the opportunity of reducing the number of changes. Of course, corrections which are made because of printer's errors are not charged to the author at all, and some publishers are sensible enough to include a sentence saying that their own mistakes (i.e. *publisher's* errors) may be corrected without cost to the author – most copy editors are meticulous, but like anyone else they can make mistakes and will occasionally alter something in the author's script which was perfectly all right, or will make an error in their own revisions (of course, if the author is given the opportunity to see and approve the copy-edited typescript before it goes to the printer, the problem should not arise). Publishers vary in the way they deal with the excess charges that authors may incur on the proofs, some putting the debit on the author's account, and others wanting the author to pay cash. The MTA says that the sum will be deducted from the advance or royalties, but if all the advance has been paid and if there is some doubt about whether it will ever be earned and any additional royalties will be paid, you can't really blame a publisher who asks for an immediate repayment by the author.

WARNING

Since publishers usually want the proofs turned around very promptly, it is well worth asking your publisher when he expects to be sending them to you, and keeping him informed of dates when you are going to be away. Although most publishers would be reasonable about it, I think, it would be extremely annoying to go away for a fortnight's holiday and come back to find that the proofs had been sitting on your doormat since the day you left and that the publisher had regarded them as passed for press because he hadn't heard from you by the due date.

Make sure that the final version of your typescript is as perfect as possible, so that you can keep your corrections to an absolute minimum. If you can foresee that a lot of changes will have to be made (perhaps because it is essential to keep the information in the book as up-to-date as possible), discuss the matter with your publisher in advance, so that you can come to an arrangement about the expense of changes (such costs should be built into the manufacturing estimates, and so ultimately into the retail price of the book, rather than being charged to you).

PROMOTION

Some publishers include under the author's obligations a clause stating that the author will assist the publisher in any promotion of the work. You might think it strange that a publisher would want to include such a clause, because surely every author would be not merely willing, but eager to help with promotion. However, there are some authors who shy away from anything of the kind, and in such cases a publisher can use a clause of this kind to defend himself if the author accuses him of a lack of enthusiasm in promoting the book. However, I cannot imagine, except in the most extreme and angry dispute between a publisher and an author, that any publisher, in attempting to break a contract, would invoke an author's failure to comply with the requirements of such a clause as sufficient grounds for doing so.

THE AUTHOR'S USE OF HIS OWN MATERIAL

This clause is often given a different heading – 'Competitive material', or something of that sort. Publishers usually want to include a clause to prevent the author from publishing with another publisher a work which is so similar to the one which is the subject of the contract that it would be competitive with it, or to reproduce elsewhere any substantial part of the work. An even worse version of the clause uses a vague, blanket wording which prohibits the author from publishing any other work which might be regarded as prejudicing the sales of the book in question. The basic MTA does not include any such provision, whether bland or harsh, and the reason for this is undoubtedly that if you are a non-fiction author you may have a specialist subject, and it is often very difficult in such a case to avoid using the same basic material in more than one of your books – 'plagiarizing yourself', as it were – and if you are not allowed to do that, you may not be able to go on writing books on your pet subject. That could be a very unhappy restriction. You do not use someone else's material without permission, but may perhaps take from that work some basic, widely available information which you then rewrite and disguise to such an extent that it is unrecognizable as belonging to that person, and has become your own property; in exactly the same way, if you plagiarize yourself, you should try to do it with such skill that it seems totally new. But in any case, it is clearly far less terrible a crime if the book which you are plagiarizing and the new book are both published by the same firm – if the publisher accepts it, he should at least be aware of any duplication of interest. However, a sensible author does not want to harm his own sales by publishing books which compete too closely with each other.

WARNING

Don't agree to this clause if you can avoid it. If the publisher insists on it, then clarify exactly what is meant, and make sure that you will not be deprived of your livelihood (or even your pin money) by such a restriction. If you have already signed a contract with such a clause, it may be some consolation to know that the prohibition does not survive termination – in other words, once the rights in the book revert to you, you are free to publish other works which are competitive with it.

OPTIONS

The term 'option' is used to describe the right which in many agreements the author gives to the publisher to have the opportunity of publishing or considering for publication the author's next book(s). You may find considerable variety in the wording of option clauses, varying from the appalling to the inoffensive. The worst versions simply state baldly that the author shall submit his next two or perhaps three similar works ('full-length' may be inserted in front of 'works') to the publisher who has the right to purchase them on the same terms as those embodied in the present contract; that might be all right if the terms of the first contract were generous, but in most cases when such clauses are used, the contract is a miserable one from the author's point of view; moreover, this clause ties the author to that particular publisher, even if he is far from satisfied with the treatment he is given. The fact that the publisher has the right to purchase the books does not mean that he has any obligation to do so, which is perhaps fair enough, but since there is no suggestion in the clause of how quickly the publisher should make his decision, the author could be kept waiting indefinitely, and in the meantime would be unable to submit the book(s) elsewhere.

It was because of option clauses of that kind that the Society of Authors advised its members not to sign any option clause whatsoever, whether the terms were reasonable or not. Their view was that publishers should earn the right, by doing a good job and behaving generally in an author-friendly manner, to continue to publish any author on their lists, and if they earned the goodwill of the author in that way, the latter would be only too pleased to continue with them. The author would, of course, still reserve the right to ask for better terms.

Publishers were not entirely satisfied with this concept, and wanted some kind of right of first refusal to be embodied in the contract – and most of them still feel that they need a guarantee that the author will not simply go off without a word and sign himself up with one of their competitors. (It is worth noting, perhaps, that not all the villains in this business are publishers – some authors can be disloyal and generally difficult without any real cause.)

Some publishers try to meet the objections of authors by using wording to the effect that if they wish to sign up the next similar work – and they confine the option to one book rather than to two or more – it will be 'on terms which shall be fair and reasonable'. However, unless there is a further concession to say that the terms shall be mutually agreed, it is presumably the publisher only who is entitled to decide exactly what is 'fair and reasonable', and there are still other dangers lurking, as we shall see in a moment.

The MTA is brief in its First Refusal clause (Clause 26),

merely saying that the publisher may ask for the opportunity to consider the author's next work, and then laying down the time which the publisher will be allowed in order to make an offer (three weeks if the next work is submitted in the form of a synopsis, and six weeks in the case of a completed work – and these are not unreasonable periods, as the PA Code of Practice agrees, even for the more bureaucratic of conglomerates, though some publishers will say that they need at least three months, whether the next book is submitted in synopsis form or in a finished state). It doesn't impose any obligation on the author to agree to the publisher's request to see the next book; it says nothing at all about terms, nor does it mention the fact that virtually all publishers will expect that, even if the financial terms for the next book are entirely open to negotiation, the author will offer the same rights and for the same territories as for the earlier book.

You may think that this lack of any mention of the slightest obligation on the author's part is going a bit far, especially if your publisher is a nice chap and you get on well with him. But with the kind of option clauses that most publishers like, only if he turns the book down will you be sure of being free of the difficulties that can arise. Suppose you don't like the terms he offers – even if the contract says that the terms must be mutually agreed, it may be weeks or even months before the argument is over and you can offer the book elsewhere. Would it be fair perhaps to work out some wording which would allow you to submit your work to another publisher with the proviso that you would give your own publisher the chance of equalling or even bettering the offer? No. If you look at Clause 4c of the MTA you will see that this sort of procedure may be used when it comes to negotiating the extension of an existing contract, but there is a great difference between renewing a licence and drawing up an agreement in respect of a new work.

The wisest advice is not to give anything more than the MTA suggests, and if you can get away without signing any kind of option or first refusal clause, do so. If your publisher feels very strongly about it, you might say that you would give in if he could be persuaded to make you a payment in order to secure the right of first refusal.

It is perhaps worth noting that some publishers, while insisting on a firm option on the author's next book, will not consider it until a period of time has elapsed after publication of the book which is the subject of the current contract. They want to be sure, not altogether unreasonably, that the first book is successful before signing up another. The justice of their argument does, however, depend on the nature of the books concerned – it will not be valid in all cases – and, valid or not, a reasonable time limit should still be set.

As a side note, it is interesting that at least one publisher includes wording in a contract for an option book to say that the agreement results from and satisfies that earlier option clause.

If your book has been sold in the United States, your American publisher may have an option on your next work. If the original book was taken in the first place by a British publisher, you should be careful not to show the next work to the American house earlier than the British house. Simultaneous submission is probably all right, but it may be wiser to give the Brit first look.

WARNING

Don't ever sign an option or first refusal clause which defines the terms to be offered – look out especially for unacceptable wording such as 'on the same terms' or 'on the same royalty basis' or 'with a similar sum as an advance'.

Try to persuade your publisher not to include an option clause in your contract, but if he insists, make sure that as well as leaving the terms totally unspecified, it also imposes time limits within which any offer must be made.

III   THE PUBLISHER'S OBLIGATIONS

PUBLICATION

This clause will begin with an undertaking by the publisher to print and publish the work, and it will usually be 'at his own expense and risk' (or similar wording). It is perhaps worth remembering, if you are an author who complains of the way that publishers treat authors, that books *are* published at the expense of the publisher – and nowadays that probably means a minimum investment of something like £7,000 – and at his risk. Publishing is a high risk business, in which profit margins are tight (except on a bestseller) and very very few books can be guaranteed to make a profit. Moreover, general publishing is, alas, a luxury trade – reading is not a required activity for many of the population – and one which is particularly subject to the effects of recession. Nevertheless, publishers manage somehow to survive, and accept the risks involved in their business.

The clause usually continues by stating that publication will take place within a given period, which may be so many months after signature of the agreement (if the work in question is already completed) or after delivery of the typescript (in the case of a commissioned book). The normal publication process takes about nine months; it is possible to bring out some books much more quickly than that, while others, because of such complications as complex layouts with many illustrations, or editorial problems, can take very much longer. One publisher of library fiction states in his agreement that publication may not take place until as long as two years after signature of the agreement, and not even then in some cases for a prolific author, because the publisher will not bring out two books by the same person within six months of each other. Two years seems an excessively long delay, but that publisher works with a big backlog of unpublished typescripts, and the exceptionally large number of books which he has in the pipeline at any one time has to be taken into consideration. However, the normal time-lag between delivery of the typescript and publication should not be longer than twelve months, and this is the period which is usually inserted in the agreement.

It is normal and reasonable for a provision to be made giving the publisher extra time without penalty if he is prevented from publishing during the allocated period because of events beyond his control, and some contracts include a whole list of the hazards which he may meet, such as strikes, lockouts, revolution, riot, fire, flood, storm, tempest, acts of God (what an exciting life these publishers lead!).

Some publishers include in the clause committing them to

publication a proposed price at which the book will be published and a proposed initial print quantity, although, if they have any sense, they may give themselves leeway by adding that reasonable changes may be made both to price and print quantity if circumstances so demand. It is wise for the author to ask for the proposed price to be specified, even if the figure in the contract has to be altered quite considerably by the time the book is published, because its inclusion does generally commit the publisher to the format of the book (by comparing the prices given with those of books already on the market, it will be plain whether the book is scheduled to appear as a hardcover edition, a trade paperback or a mass market paperback). The same useful inference can be drawn from the inclusion of the print figure. Moreover, if the figures are included, the publisher has an obligation to inform the author, as publication approaches, what the final price and print quantity will be.

Most publishers include wording in this clause allowing them to ask for alterations to be made to the text, and this is reasonable, as long as it is a request and not a demand. The publisher may want changes because he does not consider the book to be of publishable standard, or because he believes it to include unlawful material. Of course he may feel the book's failings to be so great that they cannot easily be cured, and therefore that he will not publish it. The MTA meets these situations firstly by insisting (Clause 1b) that the publisher should give his reactions within thirty days (a stipulation which will be welcomed by all authors who have had to wait interminably for a publisher's verdict despite being entitled to consider themselves 'established' on that publisher's list), and secondly by requiring detailed reasons to be given for rejection of the script. Clearly the intention of the MTA is that, while authors should listen to and accept valid criticism, no unreasonable alterations should be asked for, nor should a book be rejected without sound cause being shown.

It is also in this clause, incidentally, that many publishers include a proviso to the effect that they will not be responsible for any loss or damage to the typescript and any other materials submitted by the author while they are in the publisher's possession.

WARNING

Watch out for contracts which either say nothing about when the book will be published or use some vague phrase such as 'with reasonable promptitude' or, worse, 'within a reasonable time' (which does not have the same suggestion of even a minimal amount of urgency). Equally, don't be fooled by wording which says that the book will be published within a fixed number of months from the date when copy-editing is complete, or when proofs are passed, or when paper has been ordered, or after any similar date which is not fixed at the time that the contract is signed, and which is not in any way in the author's control. Always ask for a clause which imposes a time limit on publication starting from the date at which the agreement is signed or the date on which you deliver the final typescript, and agree to a longer delay than twelve months only in circumstances which you either know about and accept or which the publisher can justify when you ask him about it. Tim Hely Hutchinson of Headline Publishers recently wrote in *The Bookseller*, 'There is no good reason why the majority of manuscripts should not be published within at most nine months of delivery instead of the 15 to 18 month timescales common in many larger houses.' It is vital to understand that if the contract does not contain a time limit for publication which can be related to a known date, such as that of the agreement or delivery of the work, there is no practical way in which the publisher can be forced to bring the book out.

The question of the publisher's right to accept or reject a commissioned work is a knotty one. If a book is below standard, it does nobody any good to publish it; but the problem is that the standards by which typescripts are judged are personal ones – there are no rules and regulations against which it can be measured. In order to preserve his right to reject what he considers to be a poor book, the publisher may want to include here some such wording as 'the author shall deliver the typescript in a form acceptable to the publisher' or 'the publisher may reject the typescript if it is not approved by him in form and content', or to include in the clause covering the advance such wording as 'one third of the advance shall be payable on acceptance by the publisher of the typescript' (note the word 'acceptance', and all that it implies). It is worth asking why publishers should want their contracts to contain provisions of this sort. Most agreements are signed by both publisher and author in good faith, the author intending to write a good book and the publisher intending to publish it, and nothing should go wrong if the publisher has satisfied himself that the author is capable of writing the book, and if both parties have agreed, in some detail, about its content. The answer is that even when the books have been carefully thought out and discussed, a significant number of commissioned books turn out, on delivery of the typescript, to differ considerably in content, or more often in standard, from the original concept. The plain fact is that authors aren't always perfect, and shouldn't consider themselves the aggrieved party when their poorly-written books are turned down under a clause of this sort.

However, whether justified or not, the inclusion of wording which allows for arbitrary rejection by the publisher means, as the Society of Authors must be tired of pointing out, that the agreement is not an agreement to publish, but merely an agreement to consider the work for publication, leaving the publisher free to reject the book on any grounds and without full explanation, and it has to be said that many publishers have used and continue to use this clause many times to reject books because they have found a more exciting book on the same subject, or because the editor who commissioned the book has left the firm and no one remaining there is interested in it or its author, or because they have decided that they don't want to publish any more books in that genre, or for any other similar unsatisfactory reason.

Fight as hard as you can to delete any wording relating to 'acceptance', 'approval' and the like. The Society of Authors and the Writers' Guild are adamant that authors should not sign agreements which contain what they term an 'acceptance' clause. Let me emphasize again, however, that reputable publishers, when commissioning a book, fully intend to publish it and do not look for ways of escaping from their commitments, *unless the author drives them to it by presenting them with an irredeemably awful book*. The presence of an acceptance clause, although to be deplored, may not be quite as worrying as has been suggested, but the degree of safety or danger for you does depend on your relationship with your publisher. It is vital in this respect to have as clear an understanding as possible when the book is commissioned of both the publisher's and the author's expectations, and it will certainly help if you can talk to your editor freely about any problems without either of you refusing to listen to the other's point of view.

Of course, that would not necessarily solve the problem if your editor leaves or if the management of the firm changes, and perhaps what is needed is a further understanding between the two parties to a publishing agreement, which could be set out in correspondence and would therefore survive any such changes: the publisher will agree that if he feels that the typescript is unsatisfactory, he will explain exactly what he thinks is wrong with it, and that his objections will be solely on the basis that the book does not conform to a reasonable extent to all the details about its nature which were fully discussed and settled at the time that it was commissioned, or that it has not been written to a standard which might reasonably be expected; the author, for his part, will agree to do his best to amend the work in order to meet any such objections; if he is unwilling or unable to do so, then the contract may have to be cancelled; both parties should feel, I think, that if the matter were to go to arbitration they could justify their respective positions.

Some authors, frequently bedevilled by changes of ownership and changes in editorial staff have succeeded in including clauses which say that the contract will be terminated unless the book is published under the imprint for which it was bought and/or unless the author's work continues to be handled by a person actually named in the clause; however, only bestselling authors are likely to have sufficient clout to achieve such concessions, let alone the confidence that they will find another publisher without difficulty if they have to invoke the clause.

Another cause of rejection which the publisher may cite is a trade recession, or his own firm's financial problems, and while these too may seem in some cases specious reasons for turning the book down, provided that they are genuine and not mere excuses (and the author will probably be aware of whether there really is a recession or not), the author probably has to accept them. If the contract is cancelled because the publisher is in serious financial difficulties, the author may even think himself lucky to escape from a firm which is about to go bankrupt, provided of course that he receives satisfactory compensation for cancellation.

If your book is rejected for reasons which you consider unjustifiable, you may have a case to take to law or to arbitration (although both these courses are to be avoided if possible, because they can be very expensive, unless you are a member of the Society of Authors or the Writers' Guild, in which case you can obtain legal advice in respect of a dispute with a publisher, and even legal representation, free of charge, provided only that you belonged to the one or the other of these organizations prior to the beginning of the dispute).

Bear in mind that if a publisher, for whatever reason, does not want to publish your work, it is in practice virtually impossible to force him to do so, even if you take him to court. However, if he fails to publish, even if he does so for reasons outside his control, such as the possible trade recession already mentioned, provided that you can show that the book is of a reasonable standard and has not departed substantially from the basis on which it was commissioned, you are entitled not only to be paid the full advance but to compensation in addition, and there you would find the law on your side.

Any mention of the publisher not being responsible for loss or damage to the author's typescript or other material should be qualified to cover the fact that he will be responsible if the loss or damage is the result of his negligence or that of his staff.

CONSULTATION

During the last two hundred years or so which cover the development of modern publishing, one of the areas in which authors have felt most poorly treated has been in the insistence of publishers that they should have exclusive control of all details of production, presentation, publication date, publicity and promotion, all matters to do with the sale of subsidiary rights, and so on; in many cases this control has been extended to give them the freedom to make editorial alterations to the text without consulting the author about them. Their argument has been that it is the author's job to write the book, and the publisher's to decide whether it is publishable, to improve it editorially, to design and produce it and to sell it. 'And we,' the publishers have said, 'are expert in our field, we are professionals, we *know* how to do it. For example, ask an author to suggest what the jacket design should be and he will, as likely as not, suggest something which cannot properly be depicted in so small an area, or which is unattractive, or which is too expensive – or a combination of all three. So, leave it all to us. After all, our livelihood is at stake, so you can be sure we'll do our best to get it right. In any case, consultation is time-consuming and therefore expensive, and invariably leads to disagreements – good reasons for not indulging in it.'

Even the most contumacious of authors is usually willing to admit that the publisher is capable of contributing many skills towards the publication of his book, and this includes editorial help, authors often being uncertain of their ability to judge their own work. The author has felt demeaned, however, by being totally excluded from all these matters, and treated patronizingly if he ever attempted to 'interfere'. 'After all,' he and his fellows would say, 'we write the books, and if it weren't for us the publishers wouldn't have any business. We recognize that they are making an investment and that they should have control over the way their money is spent. We don't want to usurp their functions or to be difficult, but we would like to be treated as though we might possibly have something to contribute rather than as naughty children who should be seen and not heard. As for the problems of the time that consultation would take and the possibility of disagreements, perhaps the publisher should simply build into his schedule the short additional period that would be necessary, and, yes, there may be disagreements, but if both sides are reasonable they can be resolved – in any case, might it not be better to have a disagreement which can be brought to the surface and discussed openly, rather than for the author to be left in a state of simmering discontent through lack of consultation?'

The 'minimum terms' which the MTA seeks to establish are not concerned only with financial matters such as the size of the advance, the scale of royalties, the split of subsidiary rights income – they are also terms which recognize the author's right to be consulted on virtually all aspects and processes of publication. To quote Tim Hely Hutchinson again, 'There is every reason why an author should be consulted and informed at every stage of a book's progress in a way most are not.'

Now, although publishers want to have the final say on the manner of publication, production, etc, believing themselves to be the experts in such matters and remembering that they are the ones who are putting up the money, most of them nowadays, including many of those who have not signed the MTA, are willing to grant the author some right of consultation, and if there is no mention of anything of the kind in the agreement it is worth asking the publisher if at least in some areas he will promise to consult. You may find a few cases where you will be met with total refusal – in the market for library fiction, for instance, the publisher will say that he will not grant his authors consultation rights mainly for economic reasons, because his whole operation depends on a machine-like process which cannot withstand any interruptions, however brief. If, as an author, you are dealing with such a publisher, you have to recognise firstly that you are in a buyer's market – there are a dozen other authors willing to step into your shoes if you choose to vacate them – and secondly that the unfairly maligned publishers in this part of the business do give a start to many, many authors who would not find anyone else willing to do so or capable of launching them.

In those agreements which do promise consultation, it is important to note that it does not necessarily amount to much more than being informed by the publisher of what he intends to do – publishers do not easily surrender their right to make the final decision – but merely to be kept in the picture is an enormous advance for authors. In fact, it does go a little beyond that, because, although only a bestselling writer is likely to have the right of veto (or the clout to impose his wishes), there is an implicit obligation on the publisher's part to listen and give due weight to any comments that even the less successful author wishes to make.

It seems to me that the various fields in which consultation can take place have different degrees of importance to authors. In certain areas it may make for good relationships if publishers consult authors, but few of the latter would be desperately upset if the consultation were omitted; in other matters, the concern of authors is likely to be very much greater.

I would say that the print quantity, the pricing of the book and its publication date are very much the publisher's business. As already explained, it is very important for the contract to contain some indication of both print quantity and published price, and obviously there must be a reasonable time limit on the publication date, but after agreeing to the details which go into the contract, and provided that he is informed of any changes in these matters, I think the author should leave it at that.

Many authors feel that they should have some kind of control over reprints of their books – that they should be able to force the publisher to reprint, if not in all cases, at least when the book sells out very quickly after publication. Alas, this is something that no publisher will concede, and in fact, difficult as it may be to believe, he is as eager as the author to reprint, provided that he can see a good chance of selling not only the copies which are out in the shops, but the reprint, too (and frequently, after careful market research, he just can't see those sales.).

If the author has granted the publisher the right to sell certain subsidiary rights, again it seems reasonable to me that he should be allowed to get on with it. (If you hate book-clubs, or do not wish serial rights to be sold to a certain newspaper, or softcover rights to a given paperback house – because you believe bookclubs are unfair to booksellers or you have a bee in your bonnet about who owns the firms concerned, or for any other personal reason – then do not grant the publisher the power to sell such rights. But don't try anything of the sort unless you are a major bestselling author whose slightest whim is accepted without a whisper of complaint by the fortunate firm which you graciously allow to publish your work.) However, you should certainly insist on being informed of all major deals, and you have an undoubted right to see the contracts granting any sub-licences.

When we get to publicity and promotion, which includes such things as advertisements for the book and the sending out of review copies as well as launch parties, tours and signing sessions, appearances on radio and television, it seems to me stupid of any publisher not to ask the author whether he has any useful suggestions to make, and in particular whether he can himself do anything which will enhance the book's prospects, but equally stupid of the author not to realize that the publisher has a limited publicity budget and to expect that he can be coerced into spending more than that budget allows.

Rising up the scale of importance, we come next to two matters which authors have complained of for years and years – the blurb and jacket. A publisher's blurb can sometimes appear to have been written by someone who has not read the book – it contains nothing, including the over-extravagant praise, which is relevant – and in the case of fiction can sometimes give away the surprises in the story which the author has so cunningly devised. Most publishers ask their authors to supply blurbs, but justifiably reserve the right to amend them or to write an entirely new version; good publishers nowadays give their authors the opportunity of seeing their proposed final wording. As for jackets, if you put two or more authors together, before long they will be swapping stories about the appalling jackets which some of their books have been given – ugly designs which do not seem to have any application to the contents of the book, and, especially, those illustrations for novels which present your eighteen-year-old, unsophisticated, blonde heroine as a black-haired siren of at least thirty-seven, or which show a church around which your story is set but fail to give it the spire which plays so important a part. Many authors have come to believe that the art directors and the artists who are jointly responsible for book jackets cannot read. Again, and fortunately, the trend lately is for most publishers to allow authors the right of consultation over jackets. It is important to understand, however, that you will not normally be able to exercise a veto. If you have a complaint about the design,

you will be able to express your concern and if the publisher
has any sense he will listen carefully; if your protest concerns
a matter of fact (the blondeness and age of your heroine, the
spire on the church), then he should take notice and have
the design altered, but if you are merely saying that you
don't think it's a very attractive picture or that you dislike
the background colour or that the typography is not very
legible, then you are talking of matters of taste, and the
publisher may politely brush your remarks aside, claiming
that it is his business, and not yours, to know what a selling
jacket looks like.

The one subject for consultation where the author really
does have a chance of putting his foot down is in relation to
editorial alterations. No publisher should make any textual
or illustrative changes without first obtaining the author's
approval, with the exception of alterations to make the
typescript conform to his 'house style' (this is usually
concerned with such minor matters as whether single or
double quotes are used, whether abbreviations are followed
by full stops, and so on – and even these can be altered if the
author feels strongly enough to want to change them). As I
have already suggested, most authors agree that a good
editor is invaluable, because the author himself is often too
close to the work to see either any imperfections or those
opportunities for improvement which a good experienced
editor will be able to point out, and others will admit to
relying on competent copy-editors to correct their spelling,
punctuation, grammar and, occasionally, facts. Moreover,
there is the possibility that the author has included unlawful
material in the typescript (possibly without being aware of
the fact) and he can hardly grumble if the publisher points it
out. However, even if the typescript is in dire need of
correction and even of rewriting, the publisher should still
not be allowed to proceed without the author's acceptance
of the changes. If the author refuses to allow the alterations,
the publisher would be within his rights in declining to
publish the book, but it is to be hoped that in such cases both
parties would be prepared to be reasonable and to find a
satisfactory way out of the difficulty. The MTA underlines
the importance of allowing the author to authorize
copy-editing changes by stating (Clause 7a) that the final

copy shall be sent to him by the publisher before it goes to the printer.

The same insistence on obtaining the author's approval should apply to titles; it has been known, not all that infrequently, for a publisher to change the title of a work without saying a word to the author, who only discovers it when his complimentary copies arrive. Needless to say, this is not acceptable practice. If a publisher wants to change a title he should be prepared to convince the author of the necessity of doing so, at an early stage, and if he has a new title in mind, to persuade the author to accept it. Of course, the author has a right to refuse to countenance the change, just as he has a right to veto any changes to the text. The result might be a refusal on the part of the publisher to go ahead with the book, and that in turn might mean a law suit. The author would then have to defend his attitude before a judge and convince him he was not withholding his consent unreasonably.

The right of consultation, with details of the matters to be covered by it, ought to be included in your contract, and you may also think it worthwhile additionally to insist on the right of approval in several of these matters. In the latter case, the publisher will undoubtedly wish to add a phrase which says, 'such approval not to be unreasonably withheld' (and some contracts will add 'or delayed'). Of course, publishers and authors may easily disagree over what is unreasonable and what is not, and it could take lawyers to sort the matter out. The intention of a consultation clause, however, is surely that there should be calm discussion, and a readiness on both sides to understand each other's strength of feeling and to react accordingly. A compromise is not always a weak way out.

WARNING

Although it may not be possible with some old-fashioned publishers who have not signed the MTA to have the right of consultation written into the contract, hardly any of them nowadays will refuse to discuss the matter at all. If you are forced to concede that you will not be consulted over the sale of subsidiary rights, publicity and promotion, the blurb and the jacket, beware of any bald statement in the agreement which gives the publisher 'the right to edit', and at least insist that no changes shall be made to the text or to the title without your approval.

Some contracts contain a provision (sometimes as part of the warranty clause) which allows the publisher to alter any unlawful material in the work in order to make it legally inoffensive. If the clause says that material can be changed if it is likely to be actionable 'in the publisher's opinion or that of his legal advisers', amend it to read 'in the opinion of the publisher's legal advisers' – such changes to the text of your book should be made only if backed by competent legal advice, and not just because of the publisher's own ideas. Furthermore, although the publisher might consider it reasonable that he should be allowed to make such changes, as advised by his lawyers, without any obligation to consult the author, the latter should in fact insist on full consultation in respect of such changes, and they should not be carried through without his consent.

COPYRIGHT NOTICE

As has already been discussed, the author should almost never surrender his copyright, and except when an outright sale is justified, agreements should carry a clause obliging the publisher to include a copyright notice in favour of the author in all his editions of the book and to require any sub-licensees to carry a similar notice. The notice will usually be in the form 'Copyright © Date of first publication, Name of Author', which, even without the symbol ©, provides protection in the EU and the USA and, in total, in more than sixty countries throughout the world. At one time it was necessary to give the copyright owner's real name in full, so a book could not be copyrighted under a pseudonym, though any author, pseudonymous or not, who had turned himself into a limited company could use the name of the company. The present-day practice is to assert the copyright in the author's name as it appears on the titlepage of the book.

Unless it appears elsewhere, the clause concerned with the copyright notice may also contain a provision that the author's name will appear prominently on the jacket, the binding and the titlepage of the book.

WARNING

Don't sign an agreement without a clause binding the

publisher to print the copyright notice in your name in all editions of the book (or with one which says that the notice will be in his name in all editions of the book; but of course it should be in his name only if you have sold him the rights outright, which, as has already been made clear, is not at all a good idea).

MORAL RIGHTS

The complicated Copyright, Design and Patents Act of 1988 decreed the existence of four moral rights belonging to the author in respect of work which is his copyright. They do not apply to work produced as part of the writer's duties as an employee – moral rights are therefore not applicable in the case of material written by a journalist for publication in the newspaper which employs him, whereas he would enjoy them in a novel written in his spare time. One of the four rights forbids the attribution to the author of any work which is not in fact his. A second prevents publication of a film or a photograph commissioned from a photographer for domestic or other private use. The remaining two moral rights affect all authors more closely: they are familiarly known as 'the right of integrity' and 'the right of paternity' (strangely, I am not aware of any major protests from feminists about this term).

The right of integrity protects the author against any derogatory treatment, such as the distortion or mutilation of his work in any adaptation or other treatment of it. No conditions are attached to the exercising of the right, unlike the situation applying to the right of paternity.

The right of paternity is designed to guarantee that the author will in all circumstances be identified as the author of the work in question whatever use is made of it, whether as a whole or in part. The Act insists that this right does not come into effect unless the author 'asserts' it, which is done simply by means of a written notice from the author to the publisher, who is then required to print the assertion in the first edition of the work. It is a good idea to incorporate the assertion into the preliminary pages of your typescript, just as you would a dedication or acknowledgement. Suitable wording is: 'The right of .... to be identified as the author of this work has been asserted by him (her) in

accordance with the Copyright, Design and Patents Act 1988'.
WARNING
Don't sign any form which waives your moral rights.

CONSULTATION, COPYRIGHT NOTICE AND MORAL RIGHTS IN SUB-LICENCES
Agreements should include a clause in which the publisher agrees to ask sub-licensees to grant the author similar rights of consultation, to ensure that the author's name is given due prominence on jacket, binding and spine, and to print notices of the author's copyright and assertion of moral rights in their editions of the work.

THE ADVANCE
It is standard publishing practice for an author to be paid an advance. An advance is in fact a payment in advance and on account of the moneys which he will earn from his book – in other words, an author who is given an advance is being given some (or all, or more than all) of the moneys that his book will earn in royalties on sales and in the sale of subsidiary rights before those sales have actually taken place. Most authors believe that advances are non-returnable, but it is noticeable that, while you may occasionally come across an agreement which does include a phrase to that effect, the MTA itself does not use the word; many publishers' agreements state firmly not only that if the author fails in his commitments he must return any advance paid, but that he must also do so if the agreement is cancelled for any other reason prior to publication, or that, even if the cancellation is the result of the publisher's failings, the author must repay the moneys if he sells the book to another publisher. If the cause of the cancellation is clearly that the author is at fault, or if he wishes to break the agreement for some reason, it may be fair to ask him to return the advance, and indeed the MTA provides for this (Clause 1c) if the author fails to meet a final delivery date. On the other hand, if the publisher is the guilty party, not only should the author not have to repay that part of the advance already received, but he should also be paid any part of it due at a later date or stage – and possibly

compensatory damages as well. As for the author repaying the money if he sells the cancelled book elsewhere, there is no obligation for him to do so, unless the agreement contains a clause to that effect (and if it does, the author should have struck it out before signing). You can't blame publishers for trying to get back the money that they have advanced on a book which they are not going to publish, but you should resist their attempts to do so when you are not at fault in any way. In practice, since publishers believe all authors to be financially irresponsible and therefore likely to be permanently in the red, few of them ever really expect to get an advance refunded unless the author is obviously successful and rich. However, they will certainly try, and if you have in some way done the dirty on them, they will pursue you vigorously for the return of their money.

It is worth reiterating the fact that the advance is exactly what it says – money paid in advance on account of all the sums which will later become due to the author, and you will not receive anything more until the advance has been earned, whether the moneys come from royalties on the publisher's sales or from subsidiary rights (the one possible exception being the author's share of an advance paid by an American publisher, which some publishers are prepared to regard, from the accounting point of view, as a totally separate item).

The MTA suggests (Clause 9a) that the advance should be a percentage (at least 55%) of the royalties which the author might expect to earn on the first printing of the book. Few publishers will cavil at that – it is in fact the way that most of them work out how much to offer the author as an advance. It is very often possible to beat the figure up a bit, and this may be worth doing if you need the cash badly, or if you fear that inflation will seriously diminish the value of your eventual royalties. Otherwise there is not a great deal of point in arguing about it; if you have a larger advance you wait a longer time for any earnings, while a smaller advance means the royalty payments start sooner. Many authors believe that the higher the advance the greater the effort the publisher will make, and this is true to the extent that a publisher who has paid an advance of £20,000 is likely to try a great deal harder for that book than he will for one for

98 Understanding Publishers' Contracts

which the advance is £2,000; but remember that the £20,000 book is invariably a work which he believes has great sales potential (he wouldn't have paid so much otherwise), while the £2,000 book is likely to achieve much more modest sales. If yours is a £2,000 book, although you won't be able to persuade him to increase the advance to anything like £20,000, you might be able to get it raised to £2,500, but that won't make much if any difference to the way he treats the book. In other words, substantial differences in a publisher's efforts are reflected only in substantial differences in the amount of advance paid.

Payment of the advance is usually made in parts, rather than in one lump sum. Half of the money on signature of the agreement and half on publication is a fairly standard arrangement, especially in the case of books which are already completed by the time the agreement is signed. With commissioned books the arrangement is often a third of the money on signature of the agreement, a third on delivery of the typescript and a third on publication. Other variants are half on signature and half on delivery, or part of the payment being delayed until some months after publication. It is preferable always that the payment should have been com-pleted by the time of publication, and indeed good contracts always contain a rider which says that the final part of the advance shall be paid, for instance, 'on publication or twelve months after signature of the agreement (or after delivery of the typescript), whichever is the earlier'. Although publishers may not be willing to pay any part of the advance earlier than is their normal practice or than is laid down in the contract, there should be no difficulty for the author in delaying a payment if it suits him to do so (perhaps in order that the money should reach him during a different tax year).

WARNING
The one point that you need to be very careful about in respect of payment of the advance is a clause in an agreement for a commissioned book which includes words to the effect that a part of it shall be payable 'on acceptance' or 'on approval' of the typescript. This point has already been covered at some length in the section on Publication (please read carefully pp. 84–7).

ROYALTIES

The MTA lays down (Clauses 10 and 11) specific royalties which are to be paid by the publisher on sales of various editions of the work in various areas. So, on hardback sales within the United Kingdom and Eire (which together are often known as 'the home market'), the MTA requires a royalty of 10% of the British published price on the first 2,500 copies sold, 12½% on the next 2,500 copies, and 15% thereafter. These figures may also apply to sales of the British edition in Europe if the publisher has been been granted the exclusive rights to that market. The rates are normally lower for children's books (partly because they are usually heavily illustrated, which means a payment to the illustrator as well as the author, and partly because they are sold at a lower average price than books for adults); they are likely to begin at 7½% on the first 3,000 copies sold, and 10% thereafter. (NB the MTA does not cover highly illustrated books, books in which there are three or more participants in the royalties, or technical books, manuals and works of reference, because their nature does not fit the standard pattern.)

There are also provisions in the MTA and in most publishers' contracts for variations in these scales for books which are likely to have particularly low print runs (Clause 10a), and for a reversion to the starting royalty rate for small reprints (Clause 10c), and these variations sometimes apply to both hardcover and paperback editions. The reason for paying lower royalties on small print runs, whether poetry, drama, or long novels are concerned, is purely a matter of economics. You might think, however, that it would not be justified on reprints, since most of the costs of origination have presumably been borne by the first edition; however, the cost of starting up the machines again for all the processes of production is extremely high, and it needs a long reprint print run before the royalties could justifiably be resumed at the higher rates. Nevertheless, the MTA would be improved if Clause 10c were omitted altogether, because the clause can so easily be abused, and often is. Its deletion (which would not prevent the publisher from raising the matter for discussion with the author whenever necessary) is probably too much to ask, but at least the wording should say that the royalty to be paid on short reprints will be agreed at the time, leaving the onus on the publisher not only to discuss the matter with the author but obligated to prove both that the low quantity is all that it is reasonable to print, and that the economics of that particular small print run demand a lower royalty.

On overseas sales of the hardcover edition, the MTA lays down a royalty of 10% of the price received on the first 2,500 copies sold, 12½% on the next 2,500 and 15% thereafter, with children's books again working on 7½% on the first 3,000 copies and 10% thereafter. Most publishers have moved to paying royalties on the export sales of the hardcover edition as a percentage of their net receipts from those sales, rather than, as used quite often to be the case, paying a reduced royalty on the British published price – half the home royalty, for example, and therefore starting at 5%. Lower royalties on export sales are justified by the fact that books are generally sold for export at a higher discount than for the home market (at 50-70% of the published price), and the publisher has higher carriage charges to pay, and frequently has to wait longer for his money (overseas booksellers and wholesalers often expect a longer period of credit, and can be very dilatory in making payments, and further delays result from the time taken for books from the UK to reach their overseas destinations).

The MTA leaves cheap and other hardback editions for future discussion and agreement, which is not unreasonable, because the circumstances surrounding such editions may not be easily predictable. Basically, the terms should not be worse than those for short run editions, unless the publisher can make a convincing case for paying you less than that.

Next the MTA considers paperback editions published by the original publisher (i.e. not licensed to another organization), recommending a royalty on home sales of 7½% of the British published price on the first 50,000 copies sold and 10% thereafter (5% on the first 10,000 copies of children's books and 7½% thereafter), while the royalties on export sales are 6% of the British published price (4% for children's books). It is current practice for paperback publishers to pay royalties on export sales based on the published price rather than on the price received, but this may change. All the paperback royalties usually apply, incidentally, whether the publisher is producing a mass market paperback edition or what is widely known as a 'trade' paperback (generally produced with a higher quality of paper and print, and certainly a higher price than the mass market version, but in much smaller quantities). In the MTA the clause continues by specifying the proportions in which moneys received from the licensing of another publisher to produce a paperback edition will be split between the author and the original publisher, but in many contracts this matter will be treated under 'Subsidiary Rights' (as already noted, there is some confusion about what is and what is not a subsidiary right, and which rights are included under the term 'Volume Rights', and so on, but in the end it doesn't much matter what you call it as long as it is covered somewhere in the contract and is fairly dealt with).

The terms listed above are considerably more favourable than most publishers who are not MTA signatories will give to new authors (or even to fairly well established authors). On the other hand, the whole agreement is one of *minimum* terms, and a top-selling author will probably do quite a bit better (perhaps starting with a royalty of 12½% or even 15% and rising to as much as 17½% on the home sales of the hardcover edition, while the paperback may begin at 12½% and rise to 15%). If you are not getting royalties at the minimum levels, wherever you fit into the league table, it is worth asking for them. Some publishers have claimed that to raise their payments to authors to the levels specified in the MTA will mean either a substantial increase in the retail price of books or that they will be forced out of business, but it is not noticeable that the books published by signatories of the MTA are more expensive than anyone else's, nor that those houses are on the verge of bankruptcy.

WARNING

First of all, make sure that you get a rising scale of royalties, even if the breaks at which the increases come are not as favourable as those in the MTA. One of the principles behind the MTA is the idea that publisher should share success with the author, and this has also been accepted by the Publishers Association, as set out in their Code of

Practice, so even a first-time novelist should have the chance of earning higher royalties if his book takes off. The one possible exception to the insistence on a rising royalty scale is in the case of library fiction, for which it is known, from the start, that all that is envisaged is a single printing of a small quantity of books – but even in this case, one would hope that the publisher would be more generous if the book should do exceptionally well.

Secondly, unless it comes into one of the special categories (children's books, text books, poetry, short-print-run books, etc), make sure that the royalties start at 10%, whether on the home sales or on the money received by the publisher in the case of export sales.

If the agreement does contain a clause about short-run reprints, some definition of what constitutes a short run should be included – the figure should not be higher than 1,500 for a hardcover book or a trade paperback, or 7,500 for a mass market paperback. But try to get the whole clause deleted, or at least to arrange that the royalty on such short runs should be discussed and mutually agreed.

Watch out for a nasty little clause referring to sales in the home market at high discounts (and this can refer not only to hardcover editions, but also to paperbacks) and specifying that royalties on such sales shall be a percentage of receipts rather than of the published price. This sub-clause often follows all the details about other royalties, or is, even more sneakily, added to the sub-clause dealing with royalties on export sales, although it is primarily concerned with sales in the home market. Following the abolition in 1995 of the Net Book Agreement, although the concept of a recommended retail price remains, publishers have been under pressure to give higher and higher discounts for bulk purchases of the top-selling titles by the major bookselling chains in the UK, which they then offer to the public at prices up to 50% below the recommended price. Although this has resulted in higher sales, the publishers feel, with some justice, that authors should be willing to accept a lower royalty in such cases, especially since they too will benefit from the extra sales.

The problem is to fix the royalty at a figure which the author could reasonably accept. The same percentages as on normal sales, but on net receipts rather than on the retail price, is far from fair. One MTA signatory has agreed to pay four-fifths of normal home royalties – a much preferable approach. It is also important to define the level of high discount at which these reduced royalties will begin (it should be a minimum 50% for hardcovers, and 52% or even more for paperbacks). Incidentally, many publishers would like to move to a practice of basing all royalties on the net amounts which they receive. There seems to be no valid reason why authors should object to this concept, but it would be essential for the percentage to be realistic, and there is a big trap for the unwary here. A royalty of 15% of receipts on home sales sounds generous, but assuming the average amount received by the publisher on home sales (excluding high discount sales) to be 60% of the published price, the royalty would need to be almost 17% to be the equal of 10% of the published price and proportionately higher if the average discount rises above 40%.

Many authors may feel that it is unfair to specify similar royalties for both trade and mass market paperbacks. Trade paperback publishers will pay no more than 7½% as a starting royalty (although the price is higher than that of a mass market book, it reflects the cost of better quality production and the smaller print run), but you should be able to obtain a rising royalty scale more like that of a hardcover book than that of a mass market paperback.

Watch out for any mention of sheet sales to or for use in libraries. Such sales follow the precedent set in the inter-war years when specialist wholesalers bought the publisher's unbound sheets of a book and bound them in durable covers for use in public libraries. The sheets are sold at a price well below that which the publisher will charge an ordinary bookseller, but this merely reflects the saving the publisher makes by not having to bind the books, and there is no justification for reducing the author's royalty to less than that paid on ordinary home sales.

Some publishers also include premium sales in a clause covering sheet sales. Premium sales are those made to, for instance, the makers of breakfast cereals. The books may be sold at high discounts, and the royalties will therefore be as laid down in the clause on such sales discussed above. It might, however, be worth arguing if the contract includes special clauses relating to books produced for mail order, or to any other unusual sales, on which it says a low royalty is to be payable.

RETURNS

Once upon a time (and the rest of this sentence certainly sounds like a fairy-story nowadays), when a publisher had sold a book to a bookseller or wholesaler, he had really sold it, and the bookseller or wholesaler was committed to paying for it. For many years now that has no longer been the case, and currently almost all books go out from the publisher 'on sale or return', which means in effect that they are merely on loan to the bookseller or the wholesaler until he sells them. If he fails to sell them, he simply returns them to the publisher, and if he has already been charged for them, he gets a credit note for the amount concerned. When you consider the vast numbers of books that are published and the huge stocks that even a small bookseller carries, it is hardly surprising that many of the books there do not sell. Some can be relied on – all booksellers will know pretty accurately how many copies of the new Terry Pratchett novel or of the latest Delia Smith cookery book they will be able to sell, they can make good assessments of the speed with which many other new books will move off their shelves, and they probably have a regular turnover of standard books like the Bible, Shakespeare and dictionaries. But with most of the annual output of books they are gambling, just as the publishers are. Eager representatives persuade them to order copies of this or that new and wonderful book (to a publisher, all his geese are swans), and perhaps also to order even more of the new Terry Pratchett or Delia Smith (some swans are truly royal). Inevitably some of the books which the bookseller has on display do not sell. He then returns them to the publisher for credit. The result is that although the publisher may think, at the time of publication, that he has sold such and such a quantity of this or that book, he doesn't really know whether that is true until some time has elapsed and booksellers all over the country (or, indeed, all over the world) have had a chance to return the copies that they have been unable to dispose of. Now, if the publisher had paid the author royalties on the quantities which he sent out initially (which are still called 'sales', though they are really no more than despatches), and he then gets a lot of them back, the author will have been overpaid. That doesn't much matter if the book goes on selling (although the publisher may be a little upset at having, in effect, paid the author a further advance), because eventually the royalties on the additional sales will make up for those on the books which were returned. But if it doesn't go on selling (a depressingly large number of books die within six months of publication), then the publisher has lost the unearned royalties which he paid. He could perhaps claim them back from the author, but he knows very well that he would have great difficulty in getting him to cough up.

This problem, now endemic to all kinds of books, first surfaced with paperbacks, and their publishers proposed the solution of making a reserve against returns. Under this arrangement, the publisher would not pay royalties on a given percentage of the sales shown on the first royalty statement, and these royalties would be retained until the next royalty statement (or possibly the one after that), by which time the publisher would know whether his 'sales' really were sales, or whether lots of the books had been returned for credit. In due course the reserve would be fed back into the statement of sales, the unsold returns would be deducted, and the result would be a true account of the position, and the author would then be paid (or not paid) accordingly. Let me make it clear that he wouldn't lose any money that he had already received (the publisher wouldn't try to claw anything back from him), but he might get what amounts to a delayed payment if there had been fewer returns than expected, or would get nothing if they had exceeded the number set aside. At first the idea was bitterly resented, and agents and authors fought against it. But pragmatism won out, and nowadays it is standard practice for hardcovers and paperbacks alike. The only questions are what percentage of the royalties on 'sales' will be retained against possible returns, and for how long. The MTA (Clause 12) suggests 10% for hardbacks, to be retained for two complete royalty periods, so that in most cases the reserve will be fed back within eighteen months of first publication, and 20% for paperbacks, to be retained for three complete royalty periods, meaning a possible retention for two years. An alternative method adopted by some publishers is to put the reserve back in stages, so that, say, half the reserve goes back into the pot in the second royalty period after publication and the remainder in the third. There's little point in grumbling about reserves against returns – they're a fact of life, and even bestsellers are affected. Publishers can't refuse to take back unsold books, but are naturally reluctant to hurry the process, which is why it lasts over a number of royalty periods.

WARNING

Some publishers may insist in their contracts on much more stringent policies towards returns than those of the MTA. They are likely to ask to set aside a substantially higher proportion of the sales and to keep such reserves for much longer periods. They may even attempt to avoid committing themselves to a date when the reserves will be fed back into the royalty computer. There is certainly considerable justice in claims that the MTA's percentages are much too low. Hardcover returns, for instance, regularly run at 40% and often higher, and the paperback situation is undoubtedly worse. On the other hand, the retention of the moneys for two royalty periods in the one case, and three in the other should certainly be long enough, unless there are some special circumstances, in which case the publisher and the author may come to an understanding on the matter. Listen to what the publisher has to say, but don't give in too easily.

Don't accept a clause in the contract which suggests that the publisher can go on making fresh reserves against returns with each new royalty period. The convention is that one reserve is made in the first royalty period after publication, and that's it, though it may be reasonable to agree that the publisher may make a fresh reserve if the book is reissued in a new edition. But of course he should seek your consent to do so.

Whatever percentage the agreement specifies and for whatever length of time the reserves may be held, do ensure if you can that the contract makes it clear that, after the period for which the reserve may be retained, the publisher will accept responsibility for any further returns (or returns in excess of the quantity reserved), even if this means that you have received an overpayment. Check your royalty statements to make sure that he is adhering to this part of the bargain.

Watch out for a clause which, having specified reasonable percentages of sales to be reserved against returns, then goes on to say that the percentages may be varied according to market conditions. That might turn out to save the publisher from paying you a lot of money which you hadn't earned, which is fair enough, but it might be used by an unscrupulous publisher to your disadvantage. Don't accept such a clause unless it also includes wording compelling the publisher to seek your prior agreement for any such changes.

ROYALTY FREE COPIES

It is usual to include a clause which states that no royalties will be payable on the author's complimentary copies, or on any other copies which the publisher may give away (usually for publicity purposes), or on review copies, or returns, or any which may be destroyed by fire, water or in transit. I am never quite sure why this clause has to be included, since it is normal to state quite clearly elsewhere that royalties are payable on *sales*, and none of the copies described above are sales.

ROYALTIES AND OTHER PAYMENTS RESULTING FROM THE SALE OF SUBSIDIARY RIGHTS

Most contracts specify the split between the publisher and the author of any moneys received from subsidiary licensees. Not surprisingly, the splits shown in the MTA (Clauses 15, 16, 17 and 18) are a little more generous than those which authors are likely to receive from non-signatory publishers (or, as already mentioned, which they may be offered by

signatory publishers if they are not members of the Society
of Authors or the Writers' Guild), but they should not
differ too widely. There are no hard and fast rules, of
course, and you may find that your publisher is unusually
generous on certain rights and particularly mean on others
(as already suggested, beware of seeming generosity, which
is often accompanied by harshness in some other direc-
tion).

It is worth noting perhaps that if you have granted the
publisher the right to sell various subsidiary rights, the
contract will be between the publisher and the sub-licensee;
with the possible exception of film rights, when the producers sometimes require the author to sign the agreement, the
author will not be involved, although the contract should
provide that he will be consulted (or, at the very least
informed) regarding any deals, and should have the right to
see the relevant documents. Only if the author or his agent
retains certain rights is he likely himself to sign an agreement
for their sale or to have any chance of direct negotiation over
the terms. This is not to say, of course, that the publisher will
sign a poor contract – that would not be in his interest any
more than the author's.

Having covered earlier the application and meaning of
the various rights, few of the clauses in the MTA relating to
subsidiary rights and the split of any moneys resulting from
their sale now require extra comment, apart from paperback
rights, hardcover rights when they have the status of
subsidiary rights, bookclub rights and United States rights,
which will be dealt with shortly.

WARNING

Question any division of subsidiary rights income which
differs from the splits shown in the MTA by giving the
publisher a greater share. You may have to accept a slightly
worse proportion, but in most cases you should not give
him more than an extra 5% on top of the MTA figures. So,
if the MTA specifies a split of 75% to the author and 25%
to the publisher, don't let him get away with taking more
than 30% to your 70% (and put up a fight even then before
agreeing). Watch out particularly for the split on translation rights (some publishers have the cheek to ask for 50%
of the proceeds), or for the contract to make no

mention of any difference between first and second serial rights, simply indicating that all income from serial rights will be split 50/50. Indeed, that 50/50 figure has a great attraction for many publishers, who will simply say that all subsidiary rights moneys will be split that way.

It is worth noting that academic publishers are generally pretty appalling in the split of subsidiary rights money shown in their contracts, and for no good reason whatsoever. I know that it is much easier for me to say that these terms should be strongly resisted by the author than for him to risk the publisher withdrawing from the contract, but I would ask any author dealing with any publisher to be brave, and to fight injustice.

PAPERBACK RIGHTS

Although many hardcover publishers nowadays own or are otherwise linked with a paperback house, it is still possible that such houses will sell paperback rights to a mass market house other than their own, and of course if they have no close links they will be bound to sell to an outside concern, or at least to try to do so. From the beginning of the so-called 'paperback revolution', when Allen Lane started Penguin Books, and through the 1950s and 60s, when the mass market paperback business grew to its present stature, it was standard practice to divide all paperback income as to 50% to the author and 50% to the publisher. The publisher justified retaining this large slice on the grounds that if he had not taken the original risk with the book and turned it into a successful publication, and if he had not persuaded a paperback publisher into a purchase, the paperback rights would probably never have been sold and even if they had, the book would not have been a success in that form. There are still some hardcover publishers who cling to this argument and even if they allow the author's share of paperback income to rise at a later stage, start by allowing him to take only 50%, despite the fact that the 60/40 split is now accepted very widely indeed, and can be regarded as standard practice.

WARNING

If your publisher is a dodo who thinks that paperback moneys should be split 50/50, argue fiercely. You are entitled to more. Note also that the fact that your hardcover publisher is part of a publishing conglomerate and sells your book to a paperback concern in the same group does not entitle him to pretend that he can pay you only 50% of the moneys; demand a starting split of 60/40 in your favour and a rising scale according to the paperback sales and income.

Be on your guard too against a publisher who is still using a now-outdated system which, he will explain with pride in his generosity, provides a sliding scale for the author's share of paperback income based on the royalties paid by the paperback house; his sliding scale will probably begin at 50% to the author if the paperback publisher pays a royalty of 7½%, go on to 55% if the paperback royalty is 10% and reach the dizzy heights of 60% if the paperback royalty is 12½%. Tell that publisher firmly that your share should begin at 60% regardless of the rate at which the paperback publisher pays, and should rise to 70% not later than when the total income received by the publisher (i.e. before he has shared it with you, the author) has reached £5,000.

HARDCOVER RIGHTS

If you sell your book first to a paperback publisher, he may sell the hardcover rights to a hardcover house in the reverse of what might still be considered the normal pattern, even if paperback publishers sign up far more books directly with the author (or through his agent) than they used to do. The Society of Authors recommends that in such cases any moneys should be split 80% to the author and 20% to the publisher. However, many paperback publishers will ask for 50%. It's worth arguing for something better.

BOOKCLUB RIGHTS

There are two kinds of bookclubs – simultaneous and reprint. The former publish their books either at the same time as the original publisher or within nine months of his publication, and usually buy bound copies or printed sheets (which they then bind themselves) from the publisher, although sometimes, using the publisher's film from which the original edition was printed, they may print their own edition of the work. Reprint bookclubs bring out their books more than nine months after the original edition and usually print their own editions. In practice, almost all bookclubs nowadays can be described as 'simultaneous'. In either case, since they will be offering the book to their members at a knock-down price – and sometimes even for a few pence in introductory offers – the proceeds for the author will be a minimal sum per copy. However, if the sales are substantial, as they sometimes are, even minimal sums can mount up. Some authors (mostly the more successful and therefore richer ones) refuse to allow bookclub sales, because the bookclubs offer unfair competition to booksellers, because the bookclub royalties are so small, and perhaps because they feel that without a bookclub edition their own books will sell more copies at the full price. Less successful authors prefer to listen to those who say that bookclubs reach an additional market which is not really competitive with bookshops at all, and are pleased to have the extra money from the bookclub sale. Of course, booksellers continue to claim that bookclubs are harmful to them, but nevertheless manage to survive.

WARNING If the contract specifies that the author is to receive 10% (which should be the minimum) of the receipts from a bookclub sale, make sure that this will be 10% of the *gross* receipts. The Society of Authors recommends the possibility of the author receiving 50% of *net* receipts (i.e. sharing equally with the publisher the total received from the bookclub minus the cost of manufacture).

Note that if the bookclub is paying royalties, these should be split between the publisher and the author in at least equal proportions, and if the sums concerned are substantial, then it should be possible for the author to obtain a larger share after some suitable figure has been reached.

UNITED STATES RIGHTS

As with bookclubs, United States deals can be either arranged on the basis of the United States publisher manufacturing his own edition of the work, or the British publisher can supply bound copies or sheets. In the former case, the contract which is drawn up will be very similar in style (if not altogether in content – see Chapter 8) to the contract with the British publisher, and it will have provision for the payment of an advance and royalties, and for the split of income on the sale of US subsidiary rights which the British publisher has granted the American publisher the power to control. This is the normal procedure with a novel or any non-fiction book which does not depend for its appeal on colour printing. In the case of extensively illustrated books the second method is more likely to operate, with the British publisher selling bound copies or sheets of the work. Indeed, some British publishers, when commissioning such a book, will give the author only a letter of intent, and will not sign a proper contract until a deal with a United States publisher has been agreed and the colour printing, spread over the British and American editions, becomes economically viable. It is unfortunately true that US publishers, being in a buyer's market, are usually able to force down the price of sheet sales or bound copies to a figure only marginally above the British publisher's manufacturing costs, and the consequence of this is that, whether the author's royalty is a fixed figure built into the amount the British publisher charges, or whether it is a percentage (usually a low one) of the net amount received, the author's rewards are almost always minimal.

In the clause in a British publisher's contract which deals with United States rights (and in some other clauses, such as those covering Translation Rights and Merchandizing), there may be a mention of a sub-agent. Some publishers employ agents to sell rights for them in foreign countries, and in Britain when the market is an unfamiliar and specialist one, such as might be encountered in merchandizing a book. Such agents naturally require payment. The MTA (Clauses 16, 17 and 18) makes it clear that the publisher is to be responsible for paying the agent's commission on US and translation sales (but not on Merchandizing Rights), but many publishers will expect to pay the author his percentage on their net receipts – i.e. on the sum received after the agent has taken his cut.

WARNING

Don't get too excited when you hear that your book has been sold in the United States. It may be the Land of the Free, stickily overflowing with milk and honey, and while you may be lucky and make a fortune, it's equally on the cards that few of the country's riches are going to come your way. Argue if your contract gives you less than 80% of the moneys accruing from US rights, even if the publisher pleads that he has to pay the American agent that he uses. If you have a British agent yourself, and he sells US rights, he will almost certainly use an American agent, with whom he has a business relationship, to do so. The US moneys will come to him less the American agent's 10%, and he will then take his own 10% off the original sum, which means in effect that you are paying 20%. A 20% figure for a publisher is therefore fair. Of course, if your own agent and the American agent both take 15%, making 30% in all, the publisher's 20% may look quite modest. Much the same applies with Translation rights.

There may be a major danger for the author in respect of United States rights. Let us suppose that the British publisher grants US volume rights to an American publisher, who then sub-licenses the US paperback rights. The US hardcover publisher takes his share of the paperback income, and passes the balance to the British publisher, who then takes his cut, with the result that the author ends up by getting far less than he is entitled to, especially if the British publisher is naughty enough to treat the sums as paperback income and take a really large slice of them. Try to arrange a deal with the British publisher which allows you to get moneys from US subsidiary rights without having to give him a large percentage.

REMAINDERS

All publishers are optimists and regularly print more copies of a book than they manage to sell. This may sound like a supreme example of inefficiency, casting doubt on their claim to be expert in their field. However, it is extremely difficult to predict accurately the exact sales of the vast majority of books. Some are total disasters, others sell out in an unexpectedly short space of time and have to be reprinted again and again, but more often than not the print quantity turns out to be just a few hundred copies more than it should have been. The surplus stock is usually sold off at a very low price, and such sales are known as 'remainders', since they consist of the remainder of the stock. Publishers cannot always find 'remainder merchants', as they are known, to take their unsaleable books, and may then simply destroy the books.

The MTA specifies (Clause 13a) that the author will be paid a royalty of 5% of the net receipts on remainder sales, without mentioning anything about whether the amount received per copy is above or below the manufacturing cost for that book. Most publishers' contracts say that no royalty will be payable if the remainder price received is below the cost of manufacture, but a royalty of 10% of the receipts will be paid if the remainder merchant has paid a price above the production cost. However, this 10% is fool's gold, because in practice almost all remainders are sold at well below manufacturing cost, which is why publishers are reluctant to give the author even a tiny share of the proceeds. Most authors will see no good reason why publishers should not pay the MTA's modest 5% however small a price they get – after all, the alternative to remaindering is destruction, for which they would get nothing. In any case it should be possible to charge the remainder merchants a few extra pennies which would allow for the author's royalty. The MTA would perhaps be improved if it required a royalty of 10% of net receipts to be paid if the remainder price were above manufacturing cost, and 5% if it were below.

It will also be noticed that the MTA states (Clause 13) that copies of the book shall be neither remaindered nor destroyed earlier than one year after first publication. It is a reasonable provision, even taking into account the fact that the majority of all new fiction is moribund, if not dead (by which I mean that orders have ceased to come in to the publisher from booksellers and wholesalers) within six months of publication.

A complication not normally mentioned in publishing agreements is 'partial remaindering', when the publisher remainders part of his stock, but continues to sell the rest at its full price. This appears to be possible because the remainder merchant on the one hand and the regular bookseller on the other reach markets which appear to be distinct from each other and which do not overlap. The main provisions of the remainder clause will still apply, but there will be no question of automatic reversion of rights.

WARNING

It is very important to insist that your contract includes a condition that when the publisher wishes to remainder a book he should give you the chance of buying copies at the knock-down price (or if he is going to destroy the balance of his stock, should let you have any copies you want without charge) – few things are more annoying to the author than to discover the *fait accompli* that his book, which has been less successful than he hoped, has been remaindered or destroyed, so that the book is unavailable to him (unless he can find copies in one of the remainder outlets). The MTA refers to this in Clause 13 (a), but the wording would be improved if it were to say '... the Author will be given the *first* option to purchase copies at the remainder price ...', especially since he might want to buy the publisher's entire stock.

If, as is to be hoped, your publisher produces royalty statements which show how many copies of your book are still in stock, keep a watch on the figures, and when the stocks stand at much the same fairly substantial figure for several royalty periods, there is a good chance that your publisher will be thinking about remaindering. Even if your contract demands that you should be informed before the book has been remaindered, publishers sometimes forget to do so (on purpose? surely not!) and it may be worth writing to say that you would like to buy some copies if the stock is to be sold off.

AUTHOR'S COPIES

Standard practice in general publishing as far back as anyone can remember has been for the author to get six free copies of his book on publication. Thereafter he has been entitled to purchase additional copies, usually 'at best trade terms' (a phrase which has often been loosely interpreted by many publishers to mean best from their own point of view, while the alternative 'lowest trade terms' has merely meant the lowest terms that they are prepared to offer to authors), with the further proviso that copies so purchased are not for resale. The provision of more than six free copies (twelve is a better figure, or twenty of a paperback) is one of the cheapest ways for a publisher to please an author. As for the purchase of additional copies, it is vastly preferable for a discount to be specified, and it is justifiable, as set out in the MTA (Clause 19), that a smaller percentage should be given if the author is asking for credit by charging the copies to his royalty account (which presumably he will be able to do only if there is no unearned balance on the account, and the publisher will therefore actually get his money). Again, by giving the author favourable terms for the purchase of copies of his book the publisher can earn an enormous amount of goodwill, and 50% is not an unreasonable figure for cash purchases, especially when you consider the discounts that publishers give to their biggest customers. Some publishers may point out that, while the author's complimentary copies are royalty-free, he does receive royalties on those extra copies which he purchases, so that in effect they cost him even less than it might at first seem, but the publisher isn't actually losing anything on the deal, so there's no reason why the author shouldn't benefit.

The MTA replaces the standard formula 'not for resale' by saying that the extra copies which the author may buy shall be 'for personal use', the aim in either case being to protect the bookseller from an author who sets out to bypass the shops by selling his book to the general public himself. There are, however, occasions, particularly at the currently popular conferences and seminars for writers, where an author is able to sell copies of his books to a captive audience, and because a considerable element of the 'impulse buy' is involved, these do seem to be additional sales which would not be achieved in the normal way through bookshops. If you have the opportunity of selling your book yourself, especially if you are going to do so in any quantity, you should seek permission from your publisher before going ahead.

WARNING

Make sure that if there are two editions of your book (perhaps a hardcover version and a trade paperback) the contract clearly states how many author's copies of each edition you will get. If we are considering revised editions, it might be considered reasonable that, having been sent at least half a dozen of the first edition, the author should receive two copies of any new edition. Sub-licensees are normally required to supply complimentary copies of their editions to the original publisher, who should pass at least two of them to the author. A generous publisher will also provide two copies of any reprint.

Some agreements make it plain that the author's agent will be sent a copy of the work, but regrettably in a few cases the copy sent to the agent appears to come out of the meagre ration allocated to the author. Fight any such provision, insisting that the agent's copy (or copies) should not affect the author's complimentaries in any way.

As has already been mentioned in the section on Remainders, it is very disappointing for the author who wants to buy some copies of his books to find to his surprise that it is out of print. If your royalty statements include details, as they should, of the opening and closing stocks of your book, keep an eye on them. If the stocks are getting low, it may be time to ask your publisher whether there is any possibility of a reprint, and if not, for you to buy extra copies of the book (not in this case at remainder prices) before it becomes unavailable.

RETURN OF THE AUTHOR'S TYPESCRIPT

The MTA has a sub-clause (Clause 6f) requiring the publisher to return the author's typescript within thirty days of publication if asked to do so. It's worth getting it back – if you become at all successful you may be able to sell it to one of the American universities which spend their spare cash on such archives. Besides, there is an important principle here – although you may licence a publisher to publish your book and to sub-license others to produce various versions of it, the typescript itself remains your own property, and that is true even if you sell the copyright in the work.

ACCOUNTS

The publisher usually agrees to prepare statements of accounts (commonly known as 'royalty statements') twice yearly. There are unhappy exceptions to this arrangement, especially in the case of academic publishers, who often submit statements to their authors only once a year, or at best send them out half-yearly for the first one or two years, and thereafter go into a yearly mode.

The statements show all sales of the work, including sales of subsidiary rights, during the preceding six months and the dates to which the sales are recorded are usually June 30th and December 31st in each year (although some publishers choose other dates – for instance, April 30th and October 31st). The publisher also agrees to send the statements to the author, together with any moneys due to him as shown in the statements, within three months of the closing dates, which is to say, usually, by September 30th and by March 31st (or by July 31st and January 31st in the alternative example quoted above).

The three month period between the close of the accounts and the despatch of the statement is required to give the publisher time to complete the statements for all the books which are currently active on his list – several hundred, perhaps – so that they can all be sent out on the same day. Obviously, if there are hundreds of accounts, and they are to be prepared manually, it is quite possible that it will take the publisher three months to get them ready, especially since the terms for every one of those books may differ slightly, and their results will certainly not be uniform. Since, however, most publishers have now put their royalty accounting on to computers, authors often find it difficult to understand why they have to wait so long for their accounts, and more importantly for their money. Ideally, the relevant clause in the agreement would say that the royalty statements would be despatched as soon as possible after the closing dates of the royalty periods, and in any case not later than three months thereafter, and with such wording, publishers might even be persuaded to compete with each other to see which could be most prompt. Alas, it is unlikely to happen, and any publisher who tried to demonstrate his care for his authors and his efficiency in this way would probably be drummed out of the Brownies by his fellows. Publishers like that three month gap, during which they have the use of the author's money and would be very reluctant to hand it over earlier. To the best of my knowledge, almost all of them take at least the full three month period – indeed, the majority seem to make what appears to be a somewhat perfunctory effort to be on time and apparently feel that they are doing a reasonable job if they can send out their statements within thirty days of the due date. There are some monsters who demand four months, or even five months, and academic publishers are again particularly bad in this respect. Such delays are iniquitous. I am not sure that authors can do a great deal about it if presented with a contract specifying a four or five month delay, other than to make a protest as strongly as possible, but it is to be hoped that the publishers who demand this length of time will eventually realize that they should be ashamed of themselves, and will reduce the waiting period. As for those even more contemptible publishers who render accounts only once a year, and then ask for an excessively long delay before sending them out, one can only hope that their authors will refuse point blank to accept such terms. Moreover, any author who suffers delays beyond the date specified in his contract should complain (which you can do most effectively with the help of the Society of Authors or the Writers' Guild, if you are a member).

The clause is likely to contain a provision which allows the publisher not to send a statement, nor a cheque, if the amount due to the author is less than £5 (some say £10, or even £25, which is surely excessively high), the amount being held over until the next statement is due. It is to be noted that no mention of such a condition is made in the MTA. However, if you happen to have any business experience, and can guess at the cost of preparing a statement, drawing a cheque and mailing it out, plus the stationery and the time involved, you may feel that the publisher has some justification. In any case, some agreements which include this kind of sub-clause also contain wording which says that such moneys *will* be paid if the author specifically asks for an accounting.

One of the most important provisions of the MTA is the sub-clause (Clause 20b) which requires the publisher to pay to the author any sum of £100 or more arising from a sub-licence within one month of receipt. Since the advance is normally against all earnings, this applies only when the advance has been earned. In the past, a publisher might receive on, say, July 1st a sum of money from a sub-licensee, a substantial proportion of which was due to the author; this money would be included in the royalty statement for the period July 1st to December 31st and would not be paid until the following March 31st; the publisher would have had the use of the author's money for some nine months. Only in the past? No, the practice still continues, although most publishers now accept that this is unfair, and agree to the inclusion of wording similar to that in the MTA. You may, however, have noticed that the PA Code of Practice talks of sending the money within thirty days after the month in which it was received – which may mean as long a delay as 60 days. Publishers will also usually agree nowadays to supply copies of statements received from sub-licensees.

The MTA also insists (Clause 20c) that the royalty statement should include details of print runs of the book and opening and closing stock figures. It mentions a 'Model Royalty Statement' – a form which shows how all the information to which an author is entitled should be presented – which was drawn up by the Society of Authors and approved by the Publishers Association, and it is greatly to be hoped that all publishers will follow its guidelines and avoid the incomprehensible royalty statements which have so often been the norm. (A Model Royalty Statement is printed in my book, *An Author's Guide to Publishing*.)

A further standard provision of the Accounts clause gives the author the right to inspect the publisher's account books insofar as they refer to sales and sums received in respect of works by the author. This right may be operated by the author himself or by his appointed representative, and is at the author's expense, unless errors are found which have caused the author to be underpaid by a given amount which is usually specified in the contract. The MTA suggests (Clause 20d) that this amount should be £50, but many publishers set the figure higher than that. If such an error to the author's disfavour is found, any expenses involved in the inspection should be paid by the publisher in addition to his payment to the author of all the moneys which it is discovered were due but which were not previously paid. (Having said that, you might wonder why the MTA perpetuates the tradition by which the author is paid his expenses only if the error is in his favour; if there are any errors at all surely the publisher should be grateful to find out about them, and should stand the bill.) You may be in need of this clause if you have been unlucky enough to be on the list of one of the very few dishonest publishers, but it is rather frightening to learn that recent random checks carried out by the Society of Authors have discovered serious errors in royalty statements and payments, almost always to the disadvantage of the author, which come from the most respectable, meticulously honest of houses; no one has suggested or should even harbour the thought that the mistakes were deliberately made in order to cheat the authors concerned – they have undoubtedly come about purely as a result of human error, and it is perhaps not surprising that some things do go wrong, given the enormous variety in the terms and conditions which in a single firm may apply to the hundreds of books on the list.

WARNING

Authors should beware of a provision saying that royalties will not be payable until the publisher has received the moneys accruing from the sale of the books (this usually refers to certain export sales to countries which are notorious for their slowness in settling accounts). That is his problem, not yours.

A far worse horror is an agreement which contains the outrageous provision that no account at all will be submitted unless demanded by the author.

Always check your royalty statements with the utmost care. Most publishers aren't cheats, but mistakes are made from time to time.

Even if your contract states that moneys from subsidiary rights sales will be paid to you promptly (assuming the advance has been earned), you may find that the publisher's accounts department has different ideas. You may be told that the clause does not exist – or shouldn't, if it does; or you might be offered the old chestnut that the computer can't cope with such an extraordinary arrangement. Don't accept such nonsense.

IV   OTHER CLAUSES

TERMINATION OF THE CONTRACT AND REVERSION OF RIGHTS

All agreements should contain a clause specifying the conditions under which the agreement should terminate (some contracts use the word 'determine', which may be confusing, until you realize that it means exactly the same in legal terms as 'terminate'). When the contract terminates, all rights should return, or revert, to the author.

There are several situations in which a contract may be terminated. The first and most obvious is if either party fails to meet its obligations under the agreement. So, to give fairly simple examples, termination may result if the author fails to deliver the typescript or if the publisher fails to publish it. But in either of those cases, or if there have been any other failures, the offended party may be persuaded that good reasons exist for the apparent dereliction of duty, and when the matter has been put right will be content to allow the contract to stand – it is a matter of what may be reasonable and what may not. The agreement will often contain a provision to the effect that the offended party shall give the party at fault an opportunity to rectify the matter within a given period following receipt by the offending party of a letter drawing the matter to his attention and asking for the appropriate action to be taken. If the matter is not put right at the end of that period, rights may revert automatically – for instance, when the author refuses to amend, as requested by the publisher, unlawful material in his book. Some publishers include wording which says that if the agreement is terminated because of the author's failure to meet its terms, the publisher may commission a book on a similar subject from another author (which is probably fair enough, provided that the publisher does not use any material which is original to the defaulting author).

Termination can also often take place when the book is out of print in the publisher's edition. Agreements should carry a clause obliging the publisher to inform the author when the book goes out of print (indeed, good publishers tell the author beforehand, so that he may have the chance of buying the last copies). It is important from the author's point of view that a definition of 'out of print' should be included – the MTA suggests (Clause 24b iii) that the book is effectively out of print if fewer than 50 copies (if it is a hardcover edition) or 150 copies (if it is a paperback) are held in stock; without such a definition an unscrupulous publisher could retain the rights for years simply by keeping a copy or two of the book on his shelves. It is usual, by the way, for the publisher to be allowed to sell off those last 50 or 150 copies after the termination of the contract, though of course he will have to pay any royalties due on them. Rights may sometimes be expected to revert if the publisher remainders the book, but this does not apply if it is a partial remainder (see p. 114).

The rights do not normally revert automatically when the book is out of print – again, most agreements place an obligation on the author to write to the publisher demanding that a reprint should be published within a specified period, and only if the publisher refuses to comply with the demand or to propose the publication of a revised edition do the rights revert. Moreover, most publisher's agreements specify that rights shall not revert while any sub-licence is still in force which the publisher has negotiated under the terms of the main agreement – in other words, if he has sold the paperback rights, and the paperback edition is still in print, the publisher will refuse to allow the rights to revert even if his own edition is out of print. Alternatively, some agreements follow the MTA (Clause 24c) in allowing for reversion of the rights granted to the original publisher other than any in respect of sub-licences which are still in force and will remain active, in which case the original publisher will continue to take his share of any proceeds, as specified in the agreement. Some publishers accept a further concession to the author by saying that once the main rights have reverted, they will retain their interest in sub-licences for a further period of five years only.

Reversion of rights should also take place if the publisher goes into liquidation – in other words, if the firm closes down, having become bankrupt. The exception to this is if the liquidation is voluntary for the purposes of reconstruction (which, as I understand it, can happen for various technical reasons usually connected with accounting and tax procedures,which are unlikely to affect the author in any way, but could occur rather more interestingly in the case of a company whose shareholders decide to rid themselves of the existing board of directors and managers, which they can do by putting the company into liquidation and immediately setting it up again under new control). As for non-voluntary liquidation, publishers are often aware of those of their competitors who are in financial difficulty – indeed, a house which sees bankruptcy approaching will usually seek a buyer for itself – and big organizations take the opportunity of swallowing the cash-strapped smaller fry, so it is more likely that the authors will be affected by an assignment of rights clause than by one about liquidation. The situation in the case of termination because of the publisher's liquidation differs from that brought about for other reasons. Despite any assignment clause in the contract, rights should unequivocally revert to the author after liquidation, and on receiving notice of liquidation, he should write to the receiver or administrator or administrative receiver (the notice should tell him which kind of official he is dealing with) to demand the reversion of rights, to insist that no assignment should be made, to be given details of all sub-licences, to get back any material in the hands of the publisher, and to be given an option to buy any copies of his book (which will otherwise usually be remaindered). Although the author may be a creditor of the failed publishing house, there is little chance that he will get any royalties due to him, but at least the publisher should no longer receive the benefit of any sub-licences, and any moneys due from such sources should in future come direct to the author, provided that he notifies the sub-licensees accordingly.

It is rather surprising that the MTA in Clause 24a refers to the possible appointment of a Receiver when a firm goes into liquidation, but does not mention the possibility of an Administrative Receiver or an Administrator being appointed. All three officials differ slightly in their functions. It would take too much space to explain the legal niceties here, and if you were to find that your publisher had been placed in the hands of one of these officials, it would be worth consulting a solicitor (or, if you are a member, the

Society of Authors or the Writers' Guild) in order to discover how your rights would be affected. The important point is that all three functionaries should be cited in this clause.

It is usual for the provision to be made that rights will not finally revert until the publisher has received any moneys which the author may owe him. Such sums might be, for instance for copies of the book supplied to the author, or possibly for the overpayment of royalties. It would not normally apply to the advance, unless the author wishes to withdraw the book from the publisher before publication, and one might expect the MTA to add the words 'but excluding any unearned advances' to this clause.

WARNING

Assuming that the contract gives you the right to ask the publisher to reprint your book when it is out of print, make sure that he is obliged by the contract to reply within a reasonable period (the MTA gives him six weeks). Otherwise he may be able to delay the reversion of rights. Note also that the publisher should not be asked merely to 'put in hand' a reprint (it could be 'put in hand' at once, but not actually produced for a indefinite period), but to publish it within an acceptable time.

Although the grounds for terminating the agreement may be reasonably clearly spelled out in the contract, the rights will rarely revert automatically (or if they do, as provided for in the MTA, the author may not be actually aware of the fact). If you are in the situation where termination is taking place, you should always write to ask for reversion and/or confirmation thereof.

In the event of liquidation, make sure that you are given full details of any sub-licences in operation, that you get all your own material back, that you are given the chance to buy copies of your book at remainder prices, and above all, that whoever is in charge of the liquidation is aware that your rights may not be assigned elsewhere (at least, not without your agreement). Authors should be aware that dealing with receivers, administrative receivers or administrators in the case of the publisher's liquidation is rarely simple, and you will probably have to fight hard for your rights, and, if you do not have an agent, may need professional help.

If your contract follows the MTA Termination Clause as

printed earlier in this book, you may have problems in respect of any sub-licences if the main contract is cancelled because of the publisher's failure to adhere to the terms of the agreement or because he goes into liquidation. The trouble is that Clause 24c of the MTA is less than clear. It says, in part, 'Termination under (a) or (b) shall be without prejudice to ... any sub-licences properly granted by the Publisher ...' This is fine if termination takes place under '(b)', the work being permanently out of print, but if it takes place under '(a)' because of the publisher's failure to adhere to the contract, the publisher might argue that he could continue to share any sub-licence income, which is hardly fair if he has broken the contract, and if termination takes place under '(a)' because the publisher has gone into liquidation, whoever is directing the affairs of the failed company might try to use that part of the clause to justify a refusal to allow the author to direct that all moneys from sub-licences should come to him, rather than going to reduce the liquidated publisher's debt to his bank, which again is hardly fair. Clause 24c(ii) does cover the point by not citing termination under '(a)', but, as I say, it is far from clear.

Be careful that if there is a sub-clause stating that rights will not revert until the author has paid any moneys owing to the publisher it does not specify that any unearned part of the advance will have to be re-paid nor that the author will be under any obligation to buy any part of the book's production material from the publisher.

After reversion of rights for whatever reason (even the publisher's negligence), although you regain total control of your work, you do not have the right to use anything for which the publisher has paid, such as illustrations, layout, typesetting, jacket design, etc, and even if you have shared costs for, let us say, permissions or an index, you would have to negotiate with the publisher and obtain his agreement, perhaps paying a fee, before using any of that material when bringing the book out again. In some cases the publisher might be prepared to sell it to you if you wish to buy it.

ASSIGNMENT OF RIGHTS
In discussing the Preamble to an agreement I have pointed out the potential problems in giving a publisher the right to

pass the benefit of an agreement to his assigns without needing to obtain the author's permission. The MTA includes a clause prohibiting the publisher from doing so, and it is worth trying to get such wording inserted in any agreement you sign – indeed, it is something that you should insist on. Publishers are well aware of the uncertain nature of their business, and of the fact that they may be taken over and expected to assign all the rights they have, and for this reason such a clause will almost certainly go on to say 'such consent not to be unreasonably withheld'. Exactly how 'unreasonably' is to be defined in this context is a difficult matter; if your rights are being assigned to a person or organization which is not a publisher, it would not be unreasonable to withhold your agreement; but if the firm is to be taken over by another publishing house, the publisher may see his assignee as his saviour – the person or organization who is going to take over his firm, inject capital into it, and benignly allow it to continue its life – while you may see only a ruthless wheeler-dealer tycoon of whose activities you strongly disapprove. In such a case you might need to go to arbitration, and the end of the affair might be that you would sever your links with the publisher and get your rights back, which is fine if you have another publisher eager to take you and your books on, but less fine if you haven't. You may have to cope with a nasty moral dilemma.

Although it is unlikely that a publisher would have as strong reasons for objecting to your assignees as you might have to his, he might say that if a clause is included prohibiting assignment without consent it should apply to you as well as to him, which seems fair.

ACTIONS FOR INFRINGEMENT

This clause is sometimes attached to the Warranty Clause, and is concerned with the fact that proceedings against a person or persons infringing the copyright or any rights granted under the contract may be started by the author or the publisher separately or by both working together. Normally, it will be the publisher who first becomes aware of the infringement of rights, and he has a responsibility to inform the author. Thereafter, it is expected that the author will agree to take action. Co-operation is clearly desirable, but the clause usually gives the publisher the right to take action in his own name if the author declines to do so, and to join the author with him; alternatively, it allows the publisher to join in any action initiated by the author. In the former case, the publisher should agree to guarantee the author against any financial loss that he might incur as a result of the proceedings, but if the publisher receives damages from the guilty party, then he is entitled to keep 100% of those moneys; on the other hand, if the author agrees to take action, it is usual for them to share the costs in mutually agreed proportions, and to split any damages received in the same shares.

The most frequent examples of infringement are cases of piracy – publication of the book in unauthorized editions, without payment of fees or royalties – a regular occurrence in certain Far Eastern countries, although piracy is not confined to that part of the world. It is not at all easy to prevent piracy or to take action against the pirates.

On the other hand, if the infringement involves two British publishers, when it is likely that copyright material published by one of them has been used without permission in a book published by the other, a case can easily be brought. Any action that you and your publisher take against someone who has infringed your rights in any way, whether the offence is of major or minor proportions, or any defence that you make against a claim that your work is an infringement of someone else's copyright, must rest on the validity of your depositions set out in the warranty clause.

WARNING

This is an important clause, so make sure that you understand it, and do be absolutely confident that the warranties you have given earlier in the contract can be relied upon.

INSURANCE

Some publishers take out insurance against a variety of damaging possibilities which might include not only the penalties resulting from publishing a libellous work or one which infringes other persons' copyright, but also the expenses incurred in defending such cases, whatever the final verdict might be. If they have done so, they may include a clause in the agreement to set out the responsibilities of the author and themselves in the light of the insurance policy. Sometimes the clause dealing with actions for infringement is considerably extended to cover the matter.

The insurance clause is likely to contain a commitment on the publisher's part to include the author in any insurance which he takes out in respect of the book (the policy will also cover the printer and, of course, himself), but will point out that the insurance will only be valid if the statements in the warranty clause, which the author is signing as part of the contract, are factual – in other words, if the author can swear that, at least to the best of his knowledge, the book contains no unlawful matter of any kind. The clause will then go on to give details of how the author's promise to indemnify the publisher (as specified in the warranty clause) will be reduced in financial terms by the effect of the insurance.

WARNING

Not all publishers take out insurance against legal problems with their books. It is generally an extremely expensive business, and the terms and conditions of the policies are usually complex in the extreme. Don't worry if your publisher does not have a general insurance policy of this kind – if you tell him frankly of any legal problems which might result from the publication of your book, he will probably seek legal advice about the dangers. If counsel gives the opinion that the book is safe, it may be possible for the publisher or for you to take out a specific insurance for it. However, if your publisher does have a general insurance policy, it will probably be mentioned in his standard agreement, and perhaps attached to it, and you must study the terms carefully and make sure that they are acceptable to you. But don't ever believe that it gives you freedom to incorporate unlawful material of any kind in your book. If your publisher does carry insurance against legal problems, find out how it affects you.

TRADE MARK PROTECTION

In some agreements, most often those for children's books, but also for any book in connection with which the merchandizing rights are particularly likely to be sold, you may find a clause which is concerned with the protection of the trademarks which can derive from the book. Usually it says that the author and the publisher will share in such costs.

WARNING

Obtaining trade mark protection throughout the world is an enormously costly business, because it involves international lawyers, whose services do not come cheaply. It may be very necessary to protect your interests in this way, but you should insist, before your publisher embarks on the exercise, on finding out exactly what it is going to cost you.

ADVERTISEMENTS

The basic MTA includes a clause (Clause 25) stating that the publisher will not include any advertisements in his editions of the work, except for other books on his list (and will, as far as he is able, extend the condition to any sub-licensees), without the consent of the author. Not all signatories of the MTA have accepted this clause, presumably feeling that at some future date they may be driven to an attempt to decrease their costs by accepting outside advertisements. During the 1930s and 40s advertisements in books were quite common. Nobody seemed to object then, and you might wonder why they should nowadays, especially since it is in the interests of authors that publishers should not lose money on the books they publish. However, the thought behind the clause becomes more understandable once you consider how many services and products might be considered objectionable by authors with strong beliefs, whether political, religious, environmental or otherwise potentially controversial.

WARNING

If your publisher does not include this clause in his agreement, it might be worth your while to write to him to get confirmation that he will not include advertisements without your consent.

ARBITRATION

It is always to be hoped that no disputes will occur between the author and the publisher. If they do, and the parties cannot themselves resolve the problem, it will be necessary to go to arbitration. The MTA suggests (Clause 28) that a single arbitrator, acceptable to both the author and the publisher, should be appointed, and that his decision should be final. However, it may be difficult for the parties to agree on a suitable single arbitrator (for instance, the publisher might suggest using the Publishers Association's Informal Disputes Settlement Scheme, but despite its undoubted evenhandedness, many authors would feel that they might not receive an entirely unbiased hearing in that quarter). Some contracts suggest that the publisher and the author should each appoint someone, presumably in the hope that these two arbitrators, being somewhat removed from the heat of battle, as it were, will be able to find an answer on which they both agree. Whether there is one arbitrator or two, in the event that no decision is reached, most agreements specify that the matter shall then become subject to arbitration as laid down in the Arbitration Act of 1950 (or any amending or substituted statute which may be in force), and this will usually mean that an official, government-sponsored and legally trained arbitrator will be appointed.

ENGLISH LAW

Most British agreements contain a statement that the wording will be interpreted in accordance with the laws of England (or, if the publisher is a Scottish house, the laws of Scotland). This may be taken for granted in most cases, since any dispute is likely to take place within the country of origin, and no one will expect any deviation from the laws of that country. However, there can be instances of English or Scottish contracts being the subject of legal argument in foreign countries, and it is then just as well to know the legal framework on which the agreement was drawn up.

In some agreements the statement is made in a separate clause, but it may sometimes be included in the clause dealing with arbitration or with actions for infringement.

INCOME TAX

Some agreements include a clause making it plain that the author is entirely responsible for accounting to the Inland Revenue and paying any tax due in respect of any sums he receives under the contract.

There may also be a statement covering the payment of VAT, which requires the author, if he is registered for VAT, to notify the publisher, giving his VAT registration number; otherwise, payments are made exclusive of VAT.

AGENCY

Although most literary agents like to use their own forms of contract, they are sometimes willing to use the publisher's standard agreement, especially if the publisher is a signatory of the MTA. In such cases, a clause will be added specifying that all payments under the contract will be made to the author's agent (whose name and address will then be given), and that the agent's receipt for such payments shall be regarded as proof that the author has received the moneys in question. This clause may also state that on publication the agent will be sent a complimentary copy of the work.

HEADINGS

For the purpose of clarification, some agreements carry a clause stating that the headings used for clauses throughout the contract are intended only as a kind of simple guide to the contents of the clauses and do not in themselves affect the legal meanings of the clauses. Not all publishers use headings for the clauses – those that do, as usual preserving their individuality, rarely choose the same wording as each other.

SIGNATORIES

Some publishers send two copies of the agreement to the author, having already signed them, and ask the author to sign one of the copies before returning it to them, while keeping the other copy for his own files. Others send one copy, and only after it has been returned with the author's signature on it will they send him the copy which has been signed by them. The second method is preferable, because it makes it easier for the author to alter it where necessary (after discussion with the publisher).

A publisher's agreement should normally be signed by the author (or perhaps his heir or assign) on the one side and a director of the publishing company on the other. Some publishers expect the signatures to be witnessed, but this is less frequent than it used to be, and is not essential. Neither is it obligatory to initial all changes in the contract, but many publishers ask for each page to be initialled at the foot.

WARNING

When a contract arrives for your signature, do not make any alterations to it before discussing them with the publisher, and securing his agreement to them. Remember that it is possible to make changes, whether they are of major or minor significance and, provided that you keep any discussion on a friendly and reasonable level, there is no reason why you should not be able either to obtain an improvement in the terms or at least to get the publisher to explain and justify his reasons for refusal. It is, of course, a matter of relationships, and you may find it easy or difficult to deal with your publisher in such matters, but as long as you don't ask for the moon and as long as you are ready to recognize the point at which you should stop arguing, you will not lose anything in his eyes – indeed, he is likely to respect you more.

If you have been sent one copy of the agreement only, make a photocopy of the altered version before returning it so that you can be sure that the document which you get back with the publisher's signature has the same alterations as the one you signed. This is not to suggest that the publisher will attempt to cheat you, but simply to safeguard against human error.

5 Educational and Academic Books

The two basic principles of the MTA are firstly a fair financial reward for the author based on sales of the book, and secondly the publisher's duty to recognize the author's interest in all aspects of publication and his right to be consulted. These principles should apply whatever the nature of the book may be. However, it has to be accepted that all books are not the same, and the agreements which are drawn up for certain genres may vary in many respects from what might be regarded as the basic MTA. For instance, while authors working in the fields of educational and academic books should be entitled to receive the same kind of treatment as those who write for the general trade market, there are certain points which must be borne in mind.

Many educational and academic books are written by more than one author, possibly but not necessarily playing an equal part in the compilation of the book, and the contract will reflect this in a special clause regarding the split of moneys due to them and the procedure to be followed when making payment to them. Similarly, of course, it will be necessary to work out carefully the wording of the copyright notice. In some cases, the author(s) may be employed by certain organizations and the book may be written as part of their employment, in which case the copyright will probably belong to the organization, which will also collect any moneys due. Among other clauses which will be affected by the make-up of the authorship are those dealing with the warranty, correction of proofs, consultation, author's copies, actions for infringement, insurance and arbitration, each affected by the varying degrees of responsibility for the work which the various owners have. The problem is particularly acute, of course, as has already been mentioned, in the case of a publication like an encyclopaedia, which may have been compiled from the work of hundreds of contributors.

Another major concern is the revision of books in this category, which are very often more likely to need regular amendment than books in other categories, and it is essential that the clause dealing with revision is absolutely clear about whose responsibility the work will be, and what will happen in the event of one or more of the authors being unable or unwilling to undertake it. Since publishers of educational and academic books tend to be conservative in their attitudes, there is little hope that they will include a clause allowing for payment of a new advance when the book is revised; on the other hand, they are quite likely to want a provision that if the royalties have risen to a higher level because of large sales they will revert to their starting level if the work has to be substantially reset. Especially in the case of books with multiple authorship, the publisher is likely to reserve for himself the decision as to whether or not a revised edition is needed.

Another case which will demand many variations from a standard agreement is the educational publication which consists of a critical appraisal of a work of literature, quotations from which may make up a very large proportion of the total text. Moreover, this situation will be further complicated if the work of literature is still in copyright, necessitating the clearance of the relevant permissions.

If school textbooks are widely adopted by educational authorities and individual schools, the numbers of copies sold can be substantial, even in these days of cuts in school budgets, and the authors concerned can earn considerable sums in royalties (sums which would be the envy of many writers whose books are published for the general trade market). However, the actual royalty paid per copy is likely to be at much lower rates than those for general trade books, as a result of the need to keep the selling price down. This may sound as though the author is being unfairly exploited, but it is highly probable that the publisher will be cutting his own profit margins to the same end (as I believe he should be prepared to explain to the author). Nevertheless, there is no reason why there should not be a satisfactory rising scale of royalties, and authors should certainly ask for one. Moreover, since schoolbooks are normally printed in large quantities, there should really be no need to invoke the 'small reprint' clause with the resultant reduction in the royalty rate. Many publishers already pay royalties on the price received rather than the selling price of these books, and this trend is likely to spread.

WARNING

If you are offered royalties on the price received by the publisher, do make sure that the percentages are high enough to equate to earnings based on the selling price.

School textbooks are sold partly through the practice of sending out of 'inspection copies' to schools or teachers, and the books may then be bought. Some publishers refuse to pay royalties on such sales, claiming that the moneys are a contribution to their publicity expenses. This seems a manifestly unfair argument, and authors should resist it.

Educational and academic publishers tend always to pay less well than general publishers, and also to be generally less author-friendly in their contractual terms (especially on matters like the rendering of royalty accounts). Ask firmly for something better than you are offered – you can't lose anything by trying, and you might even win a concession or two.

6   Illustrated Books

Books for which the author supplies the illustrations

In general the provisions of a contract for an illustrated book, whether the book consists entirely or mainly of illustrations, or whether the pictorial element is limited, provided that text and illustrations are originated by the same person, should be similar to those for any other book. The author may consider himself to be primarily an artist or a photographer, but for the purposes of publication he is simply an author, and should therefore have the exactly the same basic terms in his agreement as any other author. The work will of course be copyright in his name.

There may, however, be some additional clauses in the contract, specifying, for instance, that:

The artist or photographer shall grant the publisher permission to use the photographs, drawings or paintings in publicity and promotion for the book. No similar clause is likely to appear in the agreement for the text content of a book, primarily because publishers do not normally quote textual passages in advertisements or on showcards, but they may very well wish to use illustrations in that way.

The artist or photographer shall obtain a written statement from any persons who are directly portrayed in the photographs or drawings or paintings to the effect that they have no objection to being portrayed in the manner concerned within the book in question. This requirement is clearly necessary to avoid any possible accusations of libel, which might arise, for instance, if a recognizable portrait of a living person were used as a representation of a character of loose morals in a work of fiction.

The publisher shall grant the artist or photographer the

right to include material from the book in any exhibition of his work, provided that due acknowledgement is made to the fact that the material is taken from the book. This right derives from the fact that even if the publisher purchases the copyright in the illustration(s), the original artwork (or photographs) remain the property of the artist, unless, of course, the publisher has made it clear that he is purchasing both the copyright *and* the physical illustrations – in which case he should presumably pay more than if he were simply buying the copyright. It applies too even when the artwork has been commissioned. Naturally, the publisher will want to have full use of it, for as long as is necessary, and the artist or photographer should not pressurize the publisher for its early return, although it may be possible to 'borrow' it for the purposes of an exhibition for a short period, depending on the stage of production which the book has reached. It may be advisable to include a clause in the contract (if there is one), or a paragraph in the contractual letter (an essential requirement if there is no contract), which will specify either that it will be returned to the artist by such-and-such a date, or alternatively that the publisher may retain it, but will not destroy it or sell it to another person or company without the artist's written consent.

The publisher shall insure the material against loss or damage while it is in his possession for a sum to be mutually agreed. This is a highly controversial matter, and many publishers will refuse to shoulder the responsibility of insuring the material, especially since premiums for doing so are usually very high. Nevertheless, since drawn or painted illustrative material is usually far less easily reproduced than a typescript or a photograph, artists submitting material to publishers should make every effort to persuade the publisher to take out suitable insurance.

As with any other book, it is vital to make sure that both parties to the agreement for a commissioned work of this kind know exactly what the content of the book is to be; there is an additional need in the case of illustrative material to specify, either in the agreement or in separate correspondence the size and nature (for example, transparencies or prints) of the artwork or photographs.

Books in which the text and the illustrations are originated by different persons

If the proportions and the importance of the text and the illustrations are roughly equal, it is likely that two separate agreements will be drawn up for the same book. The two parties will share the total advance, the royalties and any income from sub-licences either equally or in proportions decided by the relative standing of the author or the illustrator – a 'big name' will obviously expect to take the lion's share. All other provisions of a standard contract should remain the same, though the illustrator's contract may include the clauses mentioned above which apply in the case of an illustrator who is in fact the sole author. Both author and illustrator should be named in the copyright notice. It would also be fair to ask that, even if everything else is shared, both author and illustrator should receive a full quota of complimentary copies.

If the illustrations form a comparatively minor part of the book, it is still possible that the artist or photographer will be able to negotiate a royalty-based contract, including an advance, but quite often a publisher will offer an outright fee, and will expect to purchase the copyright in the illustrations. If the publisher is reasonable, he may additionally offer to pay the illustrator a proportion of any moneys received from sub-licences, but he will expect any such payments to come out of the author's share of such income rather than his own, and then the unfortunate illustrator could come up against an author who would strongly resent the very idea of giving up any percentage. It is important, therefore, for the illustrator to have negotiated a suitable arrangement with the author from the outset. Wherever he can, the illustrator should try to get a royalty-based agreement, and should if possible establish a good relationship and negotiate jointly with the author, right from the beginning, so that they can present a united front.

If the illustrator is working on the basis of an outright fee, the publisher will normally pay him either on delivery of the finished artwork or on publication, unless the illustrator is already well established, in which case he may get some or all of the money at the time of the commission. If his work is not well known, and particularly if he has not previously worked with the publisher in question, he may be asked to supply roughs, either before he is finally commissioned or at a later stage. Should the publisher decide that after seeing the roughs, or even when the finished artwork has been delivered, that it is unsuitable, a 'kill fee' is normally payable, and this will be a proportion of the final fee, the amount varying according to the stage at which the rejection decision is made.

When a publisher purchases artwork in this way, it is very likely that the 'agreement' will consist solely of a letter, and it is more than possible that there will be nothing in writing at all. Illustrators should clearly protect themselves by insisting at least on a letter which sets out the bargain between the two parties, and covers such important points as the dates when any payments will be made, details of kill fees, the copyright notice, etc.

Book jackets

In most cases, publishers purchase the artwork for jackets on an outright basis, with payment of a one-time fee. The remarks above, concerning the need to get all details in writing, apply to book jackets too, and it may be particularly important to spell out appropriate kill fees.

WARNING
It is vital for an artist whose work forms an important part of a book to get his name, as illustrator, on the title page of the book in question, since, apart from the publicity value and the pride he may experience, he will not otherwise be able to claim PLR.

Don't forget the rule mentioned above that, unless it has been agreed otherwise, the original artwork remains the property of the artist – and this applies to drawings, paintings, photographs and any other illustrative material supplied for book jackets or covers, even though the work is commissioned by the publisher.

7 Sub-licensing Agreements

It is unlikely that many authors will themselves sub-license the paperback or bookclub rights in their books, which is normally a function of the hardcover house which publishes the first edition of the book. Authors who deal with paperback houses are likely to do so only if the first publication of the book is to be undertaken by the paperback publisher or if they are selling the paperback publisher a book which appeared previously from another publisher who has now allowed all rights to revert to the author. In either of these cases they will be concerned with what amounts to an original agreement exactly similar in content to that which is discussed in Chapter 4, except that the paperback publisher may be given the right to sub-license hardcover rights (see p. 110). The chances of an author signing a sub-licence with a bookclub are particularly remote, since the whole bookclub business is based on purchasing completed copies or material for their own production of books which are then published at a price lower than that at which it is available from the original publisher.

However, since some hardcover publishers nowadays not only consult the author before signing any sub-licences but also show him the agreement which has been or is about to be signed, it may be useful to look at those points which differ from a typical publishing agreement as analysed in Chapter 4:

Paperbacks

The licence may refer to 'all paperback editions', which means that it covers both trade and mass market editions, or it may be restricted to the mass market version only. If it includes trade paperbacks, there should be a separate provision for the royalties on such editions, which should be higher than those for the mass market edition. The territories granted will almost certainly be restricted to the exclusive British and the non-exclusive Open markets (similarly an American publisher would restrict a paperback sub-licence to the exclusive US and non-exclusive Open markets).

Virtually all paperback sub-licences are granted for a restricted period – usually eight years, after which there may be provision for a renewal of the licence on terms to be agreed. Some paperback houses insist that if the licensor does not accept the terms for renewal proposed by the paperback publisher, he will not sell the book elsewhere on terms which are in any way inferior to those that he has rejected.

The publication date used to be set for all paperback editions of books which had previously appeared in hardcover at not earlier than two years after the original hardcover publication, but although in some cases the hardcover publisher may want the paperback edition to be delayed for even longer than that, because his own edition is still selling at the full price, paperbacks often appear nowadays only a short time after the original publication, or even simultaneously with it. Since most hardcover fiction has ceased to sell within a few days of publication, there seems at first to be no object in keeping the paperback publisher waiting, especially since the hardcover and paperback markets appear to be totally different as far as the general public is concerned, with virtually no overlap; however, if both hardcover and paperback are available at the same time, the hardcover publisher will probably lose out badly in the library market, now that public libraries spend more and more of their money on paperbacks, and this may be very serious for him, since libraries are the principal buyers of fiction. Whatever delay may be envisaged, the publication date is frequently of vital importance for any or all of a number of reasons, including, for instance, a project to bring out the paperback at the same time as the hardcover publisher produces the author's next book, or to tie in with the release of a film or television series. (One of the many advantages for the hardcover publishers who also own a mass market paperback house is that they can make these timing decisions to suit themselves, just as they can use the hardcover typesetting and jacket artwork for both hard and softcover editions without having to negotiate with an independent publisher for access to such materials). Another consideration which may have to be taken into account is the possible need to produce what is generally known as a 'European edition'; a British paperback publisher may seek permission to bring out an edition of the book in question for sale in Europe earlier than the date ordained for the home market and the rest of his territories, and this would be in order to compete in the European Open Market with the American paperback edition.

With the recent rise of paperback bookclubs, the agreement will probably allow the paperback publisher to licence a paperback bookclub edition.

Other clauses may provide that the hardcover publisher may not remainder his edition of the work until an agreed period after the paperback edition has appeared, and that the paperback publisher may not allow his edition to be bound in hard covers (this provision is aimed particularly at preventing libraries from putting a hardcover binding on a paperback, thus making it much more durable and at a total cost much lower than that of the hardcover book). There will also probably be a clause saying that after receiving notice that the rights will revert, or at some specified time before reversion will take place, the paperback publisher may not reprint the book, but he will have the right to sell off any remaining copies that he may have, and will be allowed to continue to do so for a specified period after reversion has taken place.

The standard clauses in the original agreement between the author and the publisher will be repeated or reflected in the contract with the paperback publisher, so the warranty (which will include a statement to the effect that any permissions for illustrations or other copyright material have been secured) and the requirement for the author's name to be given due prominence and inclusion of the copyright and moral rights notices will all be covered. A further clause may provide for consultation rights for the author if the original contract includes a promise by the hardcover publisher to secure these, if possible, from any sub-licensees. There will also be the normal clauses concerning the advance, the royalties payable, the rendering of accounts, supplying of author's copies, termination of the agreement, remaindering, arbitration, etc. The paperback publisher will almost certainly want an option in some form acceptable to both parties on the author's next work.

Bookclub

Agreements between the original publisher and a bookclub will include all the standard clauses, mentioned above in the section on paperbacks, which derive from and reflect the contract between the author and the publisher, including if possible an option. There will also be a number of clauses specific to the kind of deal involved.

In the first place, as with paperbacks, the licence for a book club edition will probably be for a limited period only, but whereas the paperback agreement will undoubtedly give the paperback publisher an exclusive licence within the British market, that for a bookclub may be either exclusive or non-exclusive (allowing the original publisher in the latter case to sell the book to more than one club). In practice, a bookclub is not usually granted exclusive rights unless the first quantity that it orders from the original publisher or which it guarantees to print itself is at least 1,500 copies, and the exclusivity lasts only for a limited period – three years, for example – after which the publisher may attempt to sell the book to other bookclubs.

The next point, since most bookclub organizations have not only a main general club, but also a number of specialist clubs, will be to specify under which of the club's imprints the book will appear. Sometimes the plan is to produce it first for the main club and later for one of the specialist ones.

The agreement will almost certainly specify the timing of the club edition, the format of the book (paperbacks have become popular items on bookclub lists) and the price at which the club edition will be offered, and if the agreement is signed before the original publisher has brought out his edition, there will also be confirmation of his publication date and price.

As a matter of interest, there used to be strict rules, applied by the Publishers Association, in respect of the requirements which bookclubs had to impose on their members to buy so many books within a given period, and the conditions under which the clubs were allowed to sell books at knock-down prices as introductory offers, but these rules disappeared when the Net Book Agreement was abolished. Another change which resulted when the NBA disappeared was that publishers no longer had to agree not to bring out cheap editions or to allow a mass market paperback to be published until a considerable time after the bookclub publication.

As mentioned in Chapter 4, bookclubs have two ways of acquiring the books for their lists: they can reprint them themselves, using setting film and other materials lent for a fee by the publisher, in which case they pay the publisher a royalty on sales; alternatively, the club can simply buy copies from the publisher's stock (sometimes the publisher will have to reprint in order to supply sufficient copies), and the royalties in this case are sometimes paid to the publisher on the bookclub's sales, or can be included in the price per copy at which the bookclub purchases the books from the publisher. The royalties paid will be based on the bookclub's selling price, which incidentally means that on books sold absurdly cheaply as part of an introductory offer ('buy any three of these books for only £1 each!') the royalty will be almost so small as to be invisible. The compensation, however, for both author and publisher, is that in some cases the bookclub will go on including the same book as part of its introductory offers for many years, and will sell many thousands of copies in that way.

Whatever kind of deal is made, the contract between the publisher and the bookclub will naturally cover all the arrangements, such as purchase price, delivery date, publication date and royalties, and the period for which the book-club may continue to sell the book to its members.

Other Subsidiary Rights

The sale of most other subsidiary rights, except those which are dealt with in separate chapters (US and Translation Rights), will usually be covered by a contractual letter or an agreement which derives from the original contract between the author and the publisher, placing the appropriate obligations on both parties, and including the relevant clauses about other standard matters such as payments, termination and so on.

8   United States Rights

If you sell your book to an American publisher you will probably be faced with an even longer and more complex document than one that you would receive from a British house. The reason for this is that the United States has a very diverse publishing trade, so there are many additional variations in terms to be covered, and also that it is the home of the corporate lawyer, who feels inadequate if he does not produce a document at least twice as long as would be needed anywhere else.

In general terms, however, the average US contract will be similar to the one already analysed in Chapter 4, and will contain many of the standard clauses dealing with such matters as reversion of rights, author's copies, royalty-free copies, remainders, arbitration, and so on. However, there will undoubtedly be a few substantial differences between a British and an American contract.

The first area of difficulty may be the allocation of the territories. American publishers do not always take kindly to the old-fashioned view which gave the British publisher the exclusive right to sell his books in the whole of the British Empire (as it then was), with all its Dominions, Colonies and Protectorates, not to mention a few other places like Egypt, where British influence had once been strong. As soon as the Empire became the Commonwealth, and particularly when some countries (such as South Africa and Malta) left the Commonwealth, American publishers began to look at some of the traditional British markets with longing eyes, whose pupils had turned, like those of cartoon characters, into greedy dollar signs. Before long they were seeking, and sometimes getting, entry for their books to parts of the world which previously had been barred to them by the wicked British (who desperately need their export markets in order to survive – a statement which is not true of American publishers, whose home market is by and large adequate to sustain the industry). Although they invaded it, the Americans did not succeed completely in conquering the British overseas market, partly because British publishers clung on to their territories, and partly because indigenous publishers in countries such as Canada, Australia and South Africa were growing and demanding exclusive rights for their home markets.

Another complication has arisen as a result of Britain's membership of the European Common Market, which demands a complete absence of trade barriers between its member states. Since in most publishing contracts for books in the English language Europe is still regarded as part of the Open market, this could mean that an American edition of a book could be supplied to a wholesaler in the EU and then reshipped to Britain, where it would be competing with the home-grown edition. The Treaty of Rome overrides most restrictions on territories contained in contracts which the author may have signed with a British publisher on the one hand and an American publisher on the other. The problem does not often arise in practice, but the only solution from the British publisher's point of view is to prevent the American edition from reaching Europe in the first place, which he can do if the author will grant him exclusive, rather than non-exclusive, rights to Europe (a move which, although they would respect such a restriction, US publishers not surprisingly do not regard with much favour, some refusing to buy the rights to British books without entry to Europe for their own edition).

Another of the territories which will immediately come under discussion is Canada. For many years it was taken for granted that if a book was of British origin and was published first by a British house, then Canada would be an exclusive market for the British publisher, while if the book was American in origin and first publication, the Canadian market would be the property of the US publisher, but this no longer applies automatically, especially since American publishers can claim with some justice that they can service the Canadian market more effectively than their British counterparts, not to mention the fact that, despite loyal links with Britain (and in Quebec with France), Canadian culture is more attuned nowadays to the American way of life, including such matters as the style of book production, American usages and spelling, dollar prices, etc. The situation is further complicated by the fact that US bookclubs expect to be able to supply members in Canada, and there is also a vigorous Canadian publishing industry which may intervene.

The business of territories has become extremely complicated, and it will be necessary to take great care in sorting out which parts of the world your British publisher may retain and which you will licence to an American house. It really is a specialist business nowadays, and it would be a very experienced, or very foolhardy, author who tries to work it all out himself unaided. Of course, if you give the British publisher world rights in the first place, then it is he who will sell the US rights, if he can, and he should be aware of all the pitfalls, and will therefore undoubtedly reserve to himself exclusivity in as many areas as possible. If for some reason you are working on your own, you will need advice – see Chapter 14.

The licence period for a US publisher will usually be the full term of copyright, but some houses will accept a limited period with the ability of the publisher to renew the licence if he so wishes.

In many respects, US publishers are less generous to authors than their British counterparts – at the time of writing, authors' organizations in the States have been trying in vain to persuade publishers there to accept some form of MTA – and you are quite likely to bristle at some points in their contracts. For instance, if your book is not complete at the time of signing a contract with a US publisher, he will undoubtedly want a clause giving him a pretty arbitrary right to accept or reject the finished typescript. Equally, you are unlikely to have any formalized rights of consultation concerning the editing of the text, the design of the jacket, the blurb, and so on. On the other hand, most authors find that their US editors, whose delight is to rewrite the original work as extensively as they can (I exaggerate, but certainly editors in the States seem to feel a need to justify their existence by asking for many textual changes), will in fact consult with them, and at length.

There will be no mention of Public Lending Right, since the United States government has not as yet legislated for such a scheme. However, PLR operates in an increasing number of countries, and it is to be hoped that eventually the necessary laws will be passed world wide. We can also perhaps look forward to a time before too long when improvements will have been made to all the existing systems; for instance, the rules current in different countries do not in every case cover authors who are not native to the country concerned (indeed, our own system does not allow of payment to foreign authors, despite the fact that British authors receive PLR from various overseas countries).

The royalties which the American publisher pays are usually somewhat lower than those current in Britain, and there will be a great variety of rates according to how the books are sold – at high discount, by mail order or premium or other methods, in addition to regular bookshop and wholesaler outlets. Moreover, US publishers rarely agree to split any sub-licence moneys at a better rate, from the author's point of view, than 50/50. A further disappointment for authors may lie in the American publisher's wish to lump together all the royalty statements for one author's books, so that royalties earned on one of his works could be offset against the unearned advance on another of his titles, although this is a point which can often be successfully contested before the agreement is signed.

There will of course be a warranty clause, but there may again be problems here because of the fact that US law differs in many aspects from the British variety – for instance, in the matter of libel. And while a British publisher who is selling the US rights may be able to insist that the agreement should be interpreted according to the laws of England (or Scotland), an author dealing directly with a US house will probably find that the relevant clause refers to the particular State in which the publisher has his offices.

9 Translation Rights

An agreement with a foreign publisher licensing him to produce a given book in his language may be presented by him to the publisher or the author in that foreign language. It is clearly preferable from the point of view of the British author or British publisher that it should be in English, and since English is the most frequently used second language, the foreign publisher may be reasonably happy to accept its use in the contract. It should also, if possible, be subject to the laws of England rather than those of the foreign country.

The territory granted to the foreign publisher will probably be the whole world, but this is not necessarily so, and especially if the book is a major seller there may be, for instance, separate agreements covering Spain and the Spanish-speaking countries of South America, or Portugal and the South American Portuguese-speaking territories. Volume rights will normally be granted, together with those subsidiary rights (in the language concerned) which will not conflict with rights being exercised by the author or by the British publisher (e.g. film rights, which you, or your agent on your behalf, or the British publisher may be trying to sell, would not be included; although the foreign publisher may need the right to grant a film company permission to use up to 7,500 words, extracted or summarized from the translation, for publicity purposes). Obviously no translation rights will be given to the foreign publisher other than those in his own language which are the subject of the agreement. The foreign publisher will expect that the warranty clause will contain, in addition to a statement that the work contains no unlawful material (and an indemnity should it prove to do so), an assurance for him that permission to use any copyright material has been fully cleared for his use as well as that of the original publisher.

The foreign publisher will be required to have the book translated into his language at his own expense, and must guarantee that it will be a faithful translation, and that no editorial alterations will be made without the author's consent. This is sometimes of considerable importance, because a particular passage, for instance, might contain local references which would be quite incomprehensible in a foreign country, but the total exclusion of which might be disastrous in the author's view. An author asked to approve changes of this sort should be reasonably tolerant – if he does not like the foreign version he can cry on the way to the bank to pay in the foreign publisher's cheque. Some contracts allow the author (or the original publisher) the right to approve the translation, but this is obviously of use only when the person who will examine it is fluent in the language concerned.

Particular care is necessary to ensure that the copyright notice in the foreign edition is correct, and the contract will provide additionally that the original British publisher shall be credited and the date of the first publication given.

For practical reasons it is fairly unlikely that the author will be given any right to consultation, other than in the matter of editorial changes, but if it is possible for him to meet the foreign publisher and establish some kind of relationship with him, then a degree of communication between the two may take place.

The royalties payable will undoubtedly be low in comparison with those paid to the British author by a British publisher, although there should be a rising scale. This is because the foreign publisher has to take into account the cost of the translation (which may be an outright sum, or a small royalty, or a combination of the two). British publishers reduce their royalties when they publish English translations of foreign language books. For the same reason, the split of all subsidiary rights is often worked on a 50/50 basis, although the author should get a higher proportion of the proceeds – perhaps 75% – from the sale of first serial rights. The advance is quite often paid entirely on signature of the contract, but this may vary from case to case. The agreement should state the currency in which payments due will be made.

The remaining clauses of the agreement will be basically

the same as those in a British publisher's contract – the submission of accounts (normally, as in Britain, three months after the end of the royalty period), complimentary copies, termination, remainders, etc. However, it is possible that the foreign publisher will require the inclusion of certain clauses which are standard procedure in his country – for instance, in some cases royalties are payable on the quantity of the book which is printed, rather than on actual sales, and in this instance French publishers will usually insist on paying royalties on 90% of the printing only, the remaining 10% being assumed to be made up of complimentary and review copies and the like.

Unless you have a considerable degree of expertise, it is advisable always to seek advice before signing a publishing contract, and this is particularly true, because of the problems which may be caused by the difference in languages and the lack of familiarity with local publishing customs, in the case of agreements with foreign publishers.

WARNING

Be careful that you understand the import of any warranty that you sign in a foreign publisher's contract, and especially, if there is anything at all controversial in your book, that it does not offend laws or taboos in the foreign country which would not apply in England.

Translator's Agreement

In the past it was usual for translators to be treated as free-lance workers who would be paid a single outright fee for the job they did, and the copyright would be vested in the publisher who commissioned the translation. Increasingly nowadays it is recognized that a translator should be regarded in exactly the same light as an author – a translator is in fact a secondary author, and is entitled to retain the copyright in his work and to enjoy all the appropriate rights and to carry all the obligations of an author as set out in such an agreement as that analysed in Chapter 4. A translator's contract should therefore contain all the standard clauses which appear in virtually all agreements for the publication of books and which are not subject to the kind of variations which may be necessary in, for instance, sub-licences, which will not be as broad in their coverage as an original agreement.

Since the translator should retain the copyright, his contract will grant the publisher a licence which the publisher will expect to cover the same territories and to extend for the same period of time as the licence which he has been granted by the foreign publisher from whom he has purchased the translation rights. The copyright notice will of course be firstly in the name of the foreign author, and will give details of the original publication, but it must also credit the translator as the copyright-holder of the translation, and he should also be given the opportunity to assert in print his rights of paternity. A further clause will ensure that his name appears with due prominence in the preliminary pages of the book (preferably on the titlepage) and it should be possible in addition to ensure that it is used in all publicity for the book. It is less usual for the translator's name to appear on the jacket or binding.

The translator will be required to produce a faithful translation of the work, and not to alter it (without the author's consent), and not to introduce into it any material which might be considered objectionable.

As for the payment, the translator can expect to receive a specified amount per thousand words. This has been standard practice for several decades. The sum is usually payable on delivery of the translation, but sometimes is made in tranches on signature of the agreement, on delivery and on publication. More recently it has been possible for translators to be given a royalty (a small one, because the publisher has also to pay the foreign author's royalties), although this will usually not come into operation until after the sale of a certain quantity of the book. The translator should also benefit from the sale of sub-licences, but again his share is likely to be small because of the original author's claims on such moneys.

10   Agreements with Packagers

As has already been explained, a packager is an entrepreneur who conceives and produces a book (usually highly illustrated, with much use of full colour) for a number of publishers whom he has succeeded in interesting in the idea to the extent that they wish to publish the book. The packager undertakes all the functions of a publisher up to the point when the book is delivered to the various publishers' warehouses. The publishers store, promote and sell the book, under their own imprints, but they do not account to the author because they buy the books from the packager in a royalty-inclusive deal. It is normally the packager who approaches and commissions the author and who is responsible for payments to him. Equally, if there should be an illustrator, he will be commissioned and paid by the packager. It is more usual, however, for the book to be illustrated with photographs which the packager tracks down from sources all over the world, and for which he clears the permissions and pays the relevant copyright fees.

An author who signs a contract with a packager is usually asked to grant world rights in his work – the packager expects, or at least hopes, to sell the book in many languages to publishers in many countries – and the contract will probably specify that the grant of rights includes all versions of the book and all subsidiary rights, other than PLR and Reprography.

Specifications are likely to be precise and detailed, not only regarding the nature and content of the work, but also its structure and length. The agreement will almost certainly say that the illustrations will be selected by the packager, but it may provide for captions to those illustrations to be written by the author (again following well-defined guide-lines as to content and length.)

Because the book is being published by a number of publishers all over the world, timing is of the essence, and the delivery clause is strict in its wording, allowing the publisher to cancel the project and to demand the return of any moneys already paid if the author is late in delivery, and this is likely to be rigorously adhered to. The period which the agreement allows for the actual writing of the book is often a short one, and, before signing, the author should ensure that it will give him sufficient time. Even if the typescript is ready punctually, amendments may be necessary, and despite the tightness of the packager's schedule, a certain amount of flexibility is normally built into it to allow for a limited amount of revision if the first version of the typescript is unsatisfactory. Many packaging contracts provide for the text to be delivered in sections at ·pecified dates, and this has the advantage of allowing the packager to see the work as it progresses and to reassure the author that it is what was required, or to tell him how he would like it amended.

Packagers usually ask for a grant of rights for the entire period of copyright, which may not be unreasonable in view of the fact that they will be dealing with many publishers, some of whom may be reluctant to take the book on with a limited licence period. However, the packager will undoubtedly include suitable reversion clauses in his agreements with the publishers, and similar details should appear in the author's agreement with him. It should also be made clear that the copyright in the text remains the property of the author and that he is entitled to assert his rights of paternity. Some packagers may suggest that the author should surrender his copyright, and that the copyright notice in all editions of the book will give only their own company name; they may also argue that the author is in effect their employee while he is writing the book and that there is therefore no justification for allowing him to retain the copyright or to assert his rights of paternity. This should be firmly resisted. He is not an employee, but a freelance. The solution is a joint copyright notice, acknowledging that the concept, styling and layout of the book are the preserve of the company, while the text belongs to the author.

A clause concerning possible revision of the work should be included, and should specify both that such revision should not be undertaken without the written consent of the author, and that the author should be given the opportunity of undertaking the work, and should receive an additional advance before commencing the job.

The main difference between a packager's contract and that of an ordinary publisher is in the clauses relating to the advance, the royalties and the payment of these moneys. (This assumes that no packager is unfair enough to suggest paying an outright fee, and that no author is gullible enough to accept such a proposition, even if the sum offered is substantial – though, alas, that may be an unjustified assumption.) An author who produces a book for a packager can expect that the royalties will be much lower than those he will receive from a regular publisher. They are likely to be in the region of 10% of the price received on the first 25,000 copies and 12½% of the price received thereafter, regardless of where the books are sold or at what discount. In fact, they are usually sold at a price which is pitched as low as possible, so that it is attractive to the customers, and which simply covers the manufacturing costs, the packager's other expenses and his profit, plus a small sum for the author. So 10%, or even 12½%, of the price received per book is not going to be very much. However, the bonus as far as both the packager and the author are concerned is that, since the aim is to sell the books to publishers all over the world, the quantities are likely to be large, so the gains can be substantial. The packager does not have to carry the normal publishing risk, since he has orders for all the copies he prints, with the result that he usually makes far more money than an ordinary publisher. And since he sells his books on a royalty-inclusive basis, the author will get his entire payment immediately (or within two or three months of the end of the half-yearly royalty period). If all the publishers who have taken the book then fail to sell it in the quantities they expected, or even if it is a complete disaster, the author and the packager have still got their money. Moreover, if on the other hand the publishers do well with the book, and ask for reprints, additional sums will accordingly be paid to the author and the packager will increase his profits.

Provision should also be made in a packager's contract for the split of moneys received as a result of any sub-licences.

The packager will usually give the publishers who take the book the right to sub-license various rights in their own language and territory, though he may insist that any sub-licence involving the printing of the book (for instance, a paperback edition) should require the sub-licensee to use the packager as the manufacturing agent for the book. In such a case the author would receive his usual percentage of the packager's receipts. However, in respect of any other income deriving from sub-licences, which the packager will have to share with the publisher concerned, the author should receive 50% of the packager's receipts, but may have to fight to get more than 40%.

It is standard practice for the packager to pay an advance against the author's earnings, and this may be the entire amount that will be due to the author on the first printings of the book (or at least, on those quantities which were settled at the time the contract was drawn up). A two-way split (half on signature and half on delivery of finished copies by the packager to the publishers) or a three-way split (one third on signature, one third on delivery and one third on delivery of copies) is also possible, but the packager may want to delay the final payment until after he has received payment from the publishers. Another possibility, if it is agreed that the author will deliver the work in sections, is for the advance to be split into several tranches, a payment being made as the author delivers each portion of the text.

In other respects the packager's contract is likely to resemble that of any regular publisher. It will have clauses covering the packager's control of the production, proof corrections, a warranty, author's copies, infringements, reversion, liquidation, arbitration, and so on. Two clauses which it will not have are those dealing with returns and remainders – since each publisher buys the book from the publisher on a royalty-inclusive basis, he does not account to the author for royalties and therefore has no need to set anything aside against returns. Equally, he has no responsibility to seek anyone's permission to remainder or destroy any unsaleable portion of the books he bought, but he will, one hopes, offer books at remainder prices to the packager who will in turn give the author the chance of buying such copies if he wants to do so.

11 Agent/Author Agreements

Before reaching the main thrust of this chapter, which is concerned with the arrangements between an author and an agent in respect of their business relationship, it is perhaps worth looking briefly at the difference between a contract for a book negotiated directly with the publisher by the author and one when an agent is handling the matter on the author's behalf.

As already indicated, if you have an agent it is more than likely that any agreement between you and a publisher will be on a standard form which was drawn up by the agent, rather than the publisher. Some negotiation over the terms and the wording of the clauses is bound to take place, and that may be true even if the agent and the publisher have a 'boilerplate' arrangement (see p. 11), simply since no two books are the same. The principal difference between an agreement in which an agent is involved, and one which an author signs directly with a publisher is that the agent's contract does not usually include US, translation, first serial and various other rights, which the agent reserves to you, and which he will try to sell on your behalf (although this is not as much a rule as it used to be, and the agent may sometimes allow the publisher control of a number of rights which he might, in the past, have reserved – provided of course that the money offered takes the concessions satisfactorily into account). In other respects the agreements will probably not be all that different from the MTA, the agent being as eager as the Society of Authors and the Writers' Guild to get a good deal for his authors, and the variations between one agent's standard form and another's are likely to be comparatively minor.

A contract drawn up by your agent can normally be signed

with some confidence that it will contain nothing unfair to you, and this is especially true if your agent belongs to the Association of Authors' Agents (membership is indicated in the *Writers' and Artists' Yearbook* by an asterisk against the name of the agency). However, as with any legal document, you should always read such an agreement with as much care as you would devote to one which came direct from a publisher – you must know and approve of what you are signing.

Having made those brief comments, I turn to the question of contracts between agents and their clients. Formal agreements are in fact rare, and many agents have represented many authors for many years without ever putting anything at all in writing on the score of their respective duties and rights and the conduct of their affairs. Increasingly, however, agents do present their author-clients with what might be regarded as an agreement, although it is likely to be no more than a letter setting out the terms of the arrangement between them, and is often a comparatively simple document, such as this:

> Dear   ,
>   *I should give you a formal note of our terms of business, which are that we charge a commission of 10% on all amounts accruing to an author as a result of any agreement which we make on his behalf and with his approval, except that on sales in the USA and in translation we charge a commission of 20% to include the commission of any sub-agent. Commission on film and tv is by arrangement, but will not normally be less than 15%. We also charge for individual items of postage over £1, and for overseas telephone calls and faxes where necessary.*
>   *If these terms are acceptable to you, perhaps you will drop me a note of confirmation.*
>   *Yours sincerely,*

This brief and informal letter may be all that is necessary between an agent and an author who have a good, friendly relationship, and who trust one another, but it may seem to some on both sides to be inadequate in these days when neither authorship nor literary agency is any longer a dilettante occupation for gentlemen (as publishing could once, in the long, long ago, have been described), but a complex and hard-headed professional business. Members of the Association of Authors' Agents are (or so I understand) increasingly using a longer, more detailed and much more formal Letter of Appointment. I am unable to reprint such a letter here, because, as the AAA points out, the circumstances are likely to vary so much from author to author than it would be impossible to present a version of the letter which could be considered as typical. It might be assumed, however, that the document would commit the agent to vigorous representation of the author's interests and efforts to sell his work, to informing him of and advising him on all prospective deals, to undertaking any necessary negotiations with publishers or other licensees, and to vetting the publisher's accounts. I would guess that it would then specify in some detail the commissions that the agent would take, including those if a sub-agent were involved, and the claimable expenses (which would include not only some postage, telephone and fax charges, but also, almost certainly, any necessary photocopying of typescripts). And it would lay down the author's commitment not to conclude any new deals for his work without informing the agent or without paying the agent's commission. Finally, it would probably set out the conditions in which either party could cancel the arrangement, and the fact that the agent would be entitled to continue to represent the author and take his commission for all deals concluded prior to termination of the relationship.

Agents are employed by authors, and are 'on their side' (although good agents also understand and sympathize with the problems of publishers), so a Letter of Appointment from an accredited agent is unlikely to hold any dangers for an author. However, if you have any doubts, you can always query the matter firstly with the agent concerned, and if you are still worried, then with the Association of Authors' Agents, or perhaps (if you are a member) with the Society of Authors or the Writers' Guild. In any case, you may be reassured by the Association of Authors' Agents' Code of Practice, which, by kind permission of the AAA, is printed below.

The Code of Practice of the Association of Authors' Agents

a) No member shall knowingly represent an author who is the client of another agency, without the agreement of such agency, whether or not that agency is a member of the Association. Failure to enquire as to an author's agency relationship shall be considered negligence and a violation of this rule.

b) No member of the Association shall charge a reading fee on his/her own behalf to an author except in circumstances approved by a majority of the Committee.

c) All members shall account faithfully to their authors, paying within not more than 21 days of the money being cleared in the member's bank account, for all sums due to their authors unless instructed otherwise by their authors or unless such sums total less than £25.

d) Members shall furnish promptly to their authors any information and material which the author may reasonably request in connection with his/her business.

e) No member shall act for an author after his/her authority to do so, whether oral or written, has terminated, except that
   i) the member shall not be debarred from continuing to act if so instructed in writing by the author and
   ii) the member shall continue to take commission in respect of agreements entered into previously with third parties by the member on the author's behalf and appropriate commission in respect of negotiations carried out on the author's behalf which are subsequently concluded by the author or a new agent.

f) No member shall charge a fee to an author beyond his/her regular commission as notified to the Association without the author's prior consent in writing.
   A member may not, without informing his/her author in writing in advance, represent in any transaction

both his/her author as a vendor of services or copyright material and any other interest as purchaser of such material and must declare to the author in writing any proprietary or profitable interest in any contract apart from that of normal agency commission. A member may in exceptional circumstances make special commission arrangements with an author provided that he/she obtains the author's prior consent in writing. Members are strongly advised to consult the Committee if they are in any doubt whatsoever as to the propriety of such special arrangement. The Committee shall have power to decide on the acceptability to the Association of any such special arrangement which comes to its notice and to require the member in question to amend to its satisfaction any such arrangements which in its unanimous view it deems unacceptable.

g) A member shall not use or communicate to others information relating to an author's affairs confidentially given to him/her except as required by law.

h) A member shall allow his/her authors at all reasonable times the right to verify and authenticate any statement of account concerning that author and shall submit promptly and regularly to the author full details of any transaction handled by the member.

i) All members shall establish a bank account for their clients' moneys separately from the member's general business and personal accounts except in circumstances notified to and approved by a majority of the Committee.

All complaints made against members for alleged violation of any provision of the code of practice shall be considered by the full Committee of the Association who shall have the right to expel any member against whom a significant and material breach of the code of practice is upheld. Such a decision shall be taken unanimously by the full Committee. Any member against whom a complaint has been lodged shall have the right to appear in person before the Committee to hear and answer such complaint. In the event of a dispute between member agencies over a matter of professional practice, other than an alleged violation of any provisions of the code of practice, the Committee may, if requested by the parties, act as arbitrators.

This Code of Practice seems to me to be an admirable document, and its clauses appear to be unexceptionable (although one would like to know the circumstances in which the Committee would approve of a member charging for reading a submitted book). The Code provides another good reason for choosing, if you can, an agent who is a member of the AAA. Of course, no one – least of all the Association – is claiming that agencies who are not members of the Association are likely to behave badly, especially since that would be to damn a number of small and/or new agencies which are not eligible to join the AAA because membership is restricted to firms which have had a substantial turnover in financial terms for a minimum of three years. However, although the large majority of all agencies will undoubtedly adhere to all those clauses in the Code of Practice which are designed for the protection of authors, if you go to an agency which is not a member of the Association you have to be prepared for the possibility, however remote it may be, that the conduct of that agency may not be beyond reproach.

WARNING

I think it would be wise for any author beginning a relationship with an agent to clarify the fact that the agent cannot expect to receive any commission on the author's PLR, which belongs to him and to no one else – unless he wanted to pay the agent for doing the paperwork, filling in the necessary forms and undertaking any correspondence with the PLR office, in which case the agent would be entitled to charge enough at least to cover his expenses.

The one other point which seems to me worth making is to emphasize the fact that you can sever your connection with an agent at any time, provided that you give due notice, but it is standard practice that the agent (who has now become your ex-agent) shall continue to take his commission on all the moneys deriving from contracts which he negotiated. Your new agent, if you have one, will take commission only from the new agreements which he negotiates. It is possible to alter this arrangement, but only with the consent of both parties.

Make sure that the details of the agent's commission are clear to you. For many decades it was standard practice for agents to take a 10% commission on those deals which they negotiated without the participation of sub-agents (who would often be involved in the sale of US or other foreign rights, and sometimes in such fields as merchandizing); nowadays, however, a basic commission of 15% is very often charged, and that, of course, although it may be fully justified by the exigencies of the agent's business and by the service that he gives, can make a substantial hole in the author's earnings, especially in the case of those deals on which a sub-agent's commission has to be paid too.

12 Permissions

If you want to use material in which the copyright is owned by someone else, you will have to seek, and probably pay for, permission to do so. Although copyright normally remains the property of the author (or artist, or composer, or other creator of the work), you will usually have to apply, in the case of text, to the publisher of the work for this permission, although if all rights have reverted your request may be handled by the author himself, by his agent, or by someone else acting on his behalf. That applies even after the author's death, for copyright continues to be in force in the EU and the USA and many other parts of the world for seventy years after the death of the creator of the work. After that it is out of copyright. So you may quote great chunks of Joseph Conrad if you want to without seeking permission (he died in 1924), but you won't be able to do anything like that with Graham Greene until 2061.

You are, however, allowed to use short extracts from copyright works under an arrangement known as 'Fair Dealing'. The short passages have to be used, so the Copyright, Designs and Patents Act 1988 says, 'for the purposes of criticism or review'. It could be argued that this phrase allows fair dealing only if you are reviewing or writing a critical book or essay on the work from which you are quoting a passage, but most publishers (who are usually in a position to grant or withhold permission) are willing additionally to allow you, under the fair dealing rule, to quote from copyright material in a way which is neither a review nor criticism of the book quoted, but which is being used to illustrate your line of argument on what might be a different subject. However, it does need to be a short extract, usually defined as not more than 400 words, or, if a series of extracts is used, as not totalling more than 800 words (provided that each extract does not exceed 300 words); if the quoted work is poetry, it should not consist of more than a quarter of the whole poem, and in any case of not more than 40 lines. Even if you are using a very brief extract – no more, say, than a couple of sentences – it seems to me courteous to ask permission to quote, and you should always give a full attribution of the material, giving the name of the author, the copyright owner (if different from the author), the publisher, and the name of the work from which the quotation is an extract. This freedom to use short extracts does not extend to their use in anthologies, for which all quoted material must be cleared, however brief it may be.

As has already been made plain, the copyright in a published work usually belongs to the author, unless the material has been written for his employer by a person who is employed wholly or partially for that purpose (as, for example, a staff journalist on a newspaper or magazine). Nowadays it is usual for copyright owners to be identified in print, so it should be simple to discover who they are, and if clarification is needed, the publisher can usually supply it. Do not fall into the trap of believing that, because material has not been published, it is not in copyright. Copyright exists in anything that you or anyone else writes, as soon as it is written (it is worth noting, by the way, that, contrary to a widely-held belief, the copyright in a letter belongs to the person who wrote it rather than to the recipient) – so if you intend to quote from someone else's unpublished material, you still have to obtain permission to do so. You also have to obtain permission even if the work from which the extract comes was published but is now out of print, and even if the publisher has gone out of existence. And you still need permission if the author is foreign, even if his work has not been published in the UK.

The situation with artwork and photographic illustrations is similar. It should not surprise anyone that an artist enjoys full copyright protection of his work, but it is important to understand that the Copyright, Designs and Patents Act 1988 has made an important change affecting photographs. It used to be the case that the copyright of a photograph which had been commissioned belonged to the person who had caused the photograph to be taken; now, however, the Act states firmly that the copyright resides with the photographer, and what is more, the Act is retrospective, so that a photograph taken many, many years ago is in copyright while the photographer is still alive and for seventy years after his death. If you have a professional photograph of yourself taken for publicity purposes (most publishers ask their authors for photos) the photographer might allow you to purchase the copyright, but will still expect to receive a credit whenever the photograph is used (and even an amateur photographer should get a credit). As with the work of journalists, the copyright in photographs may belong to the newspaper or magazine or any business concern of which the photographer is a permanent employee, rather than a freelance, and a further possibility is that it will be vested in a photographic agency.

If you have to obtain permission to reproduce copyright material of whatever kind, you should find out from your publisher for exactly which territories you should get clearance – he may suggest that English language rights in the British Commonwealth and Open Market would be sufficient (if the book is unlikely to be sold in the United States or for translation to a foreign publisher), or he may tell you that you need world rights in all languages. You should also indicate what sort of use you intend to make of the material – that is to say, what kind of book you are writing, whether you are quoting the material within your own text, or whether you are compiling an anthology, and who is going to publish it. And that last phrase leads to an important point, which is that you do not need to obtain and pay for permission until a publisher has agreed to publish your book, and indeed you may not have to pay any fee until publication of your work takes place (but see the warning on timing below).

Having written to the copyright owner to ask for the relevant permission, giving all pertinent details, you should receive back a letter, which is in fact a form of contract and which may be fairly simple or rather more formal. It may come in duplicate – one copy for you to keep, and one to sign and send back as your acceptance of the terms contained in it. It should authorize you to quote the passage(s) or to reproduce the photograph or artwork concerned, specify the territories for which permission is given and the fee payable, and state what acknowledgement is to be made and its precise form.

Although in most cases the copyright owner will require a fee, sometimes you will be given permission to print copyright material without payment, provided that you acknowledge the source and the copyright owner. This will often be true of documents which are prepared by various organizations for distribution to their members free of charge (good examples of this are the Minimum Terms Agreement printed in this book by kind permission of the Society of Authors and the Writers' Guild, and the Codes of Practice of the Publishers Association and of the Association of Authors' Agents, printed by kind permission of those two associations). However, in most cases you will be required to pay a fee. The amount will vary considerably according to the extent of the material to be used, its nature (a complete chapter or a complete short story, for instance, may be charged at a higher rate than an extract), and the kind of book you are writing. There is also a variation according to which territories you ask for; if you buy British Commonwealth rights, or United States rights, separately, the cost is likely to be about half the fee for world rights, but it could be more and if there is any certainty of selling the US rights it would certainly be worthwhile to buy world rights in the first place. A further factor may be the eminence of the author, artist or photographer – you would have to pay far more heavily to use a Picasso, for example, than a work by a relatively unknown artist, and, as already mentioned, the charges for extracts from pop lyrics are extremely high. In some cases, you may also be asked to supply one or two complimentary copies of your book when it is published (in which case, if you are very lucky, you may persuade your publisher to add to the number of free copies which he gives you), and this demand can also apply when permission is given, without financial payment, for the use of a short extract.

It is usual to make acknowledgment for the use of copyright material, in the form which the copyright owner requires, in the preliminary pages of the book.

WARNING

It is essential that you should obtain permission to use any copyright material by the time that you send your final draft of the book to the publisher (or within a very short time thereafter). If you do not do so, then you may find that, either because you cannot afford it or because the copyright owner is for some reason unwilling to give permission for the use of the material, you will need to rewrite a part of your book, or possibly to find something else that you can quote, which will mean that you have again to go through the time-consuming process of obtaining permission. Although clearance must be done comparatively early, you may not be expected to pay any fees until your book is actually published – but do not rely on this: some copyright owners may stipulate that the permission they are granting will not be valid unless you pay the specified fee within a given time (such as three months) of the date of the letter; moreover, there may be a nasty little hint that if you don't pay up within that period, with the result that the permission will lapse, the fee will go up the next time that you apply.

13 Contracts with Newsapers and Magazines

If you sell your work to a magazine or newspaper, you will probably not have anything approaching a formal agreement such as you would sign with a book publisher, and your contract is more likely to be in the form of a letter; it could possibly consist of nothing more than a telephone conversation, but even if the newspaper editor is unwilling to spend time putting your understanding on paper, you should certainly write to him to record the conversation, which will give him the opportunity of accepting it as it stands or amending it if he feels it necessary.

Most aspiring authors seem to have been well indoctrinated in creative writing classes and at writers' circles to the need to put 'FBSR' on the typescripts which they submit to magazines, whether they are articles or short stories. These letters stand for 'First British Serial Rights' and mean that you are offering the magazine only the right to publish whatever it may be in the magazine for the first time in the British market, and that you are not surrendering the copyright. Were you to send the same material to another magazine or newspaper editor after it had been published in a British magazine or newspaper, you would offer him Second British Serial Rights. If you offer the material to an American or Australian or Ruritanian magazine or newspaper for publication for the first time in that territory, you would offer First American (or Australian or Ruritanian) Serial Rights, and subsequent submissions after the first appearance of the article or story in those territories would be Second American (or Australian or Ruritanian) Serial Rights. 'Serial' in these contexts does not mean something that appears in a number of parts in consecutive issues of some kind of journal – it is simply a way, conventional to the trade, of saying 'magazine or newspaper'. In fact, there is no need, when submitting material to a newspaper, to mention FBSR, and you may be branded as an amateur if you plaster the letters or the full wording on your typescript – newspapers take it for granted that this is what is on offer and what they will buy if they want to, and they will not expect to be granted any other rights, and certainly not copyright. With magazines, however, you are on slightly less firm ground, and (even if they too think it is the sign of a non-professional) it is worth making it clear that you are offering serial rights only. Some magazines will certainly try to buy the copyright if they can – and without paying anything more than they would for a once-only use. Don't agree to that.

A letter accepting your material will probably not say anything about the territories concerned, though if you use FBSR you are, of course, restricting the use to the British market. Territories tend to be taken for granted when newspapers buy material – after all, it is fairly unlikely that a newspaper will want more than rights in its country of origin. The same is true of most magazines, but those which are truly international will undoubtedly make it clear that they require world rights.

A letter will also not usually include the kind of details that would appear in the warranty clause in an agreement for a book (though woe betide you if you infringe someone else's copyright, or include unlawful material). Indeed, the documentation will be minimal, often consisting of no more than an acceptance of the material and some reference to the payment. Everything else relevant tends to be taken for granted, which is why it is important for you to make sure in your own side of the correspondence that you make clear what it is that you are offering.

One of the major problems in dealing with magazines and newspapers is that they are often unwilling to make any definite commitment about when they will use your articles or stories. Some magazines stockpile material for many months. This is very frustrating for the author, especially if he is not to be paid until the work appears in print. If he has been commissioned in advance by the newspaper or magazine, he is entitled to put in an invoice as soon as he delivers the material, but even then, payment will probably not reach him until publication. With material which is submitted 'on spec' (i.e. without being commissioned), the editor accepting the work may say that payment will be made only on presentation of an invoice, but that the invoice will be accepted only after publication, and the problem then may be that you will not be informed (of course, you should be) when the piece actually appears, so you have to look at every issue to see whether or not you are in it.

Because an article or story in a newspaper or magazine is a one-off publication, you will not be offered royalties, but a one-time payment for a one-time use. The amount that you will be paid depends partly on your status (whether you are an established writer, or an expert in your field, or an unknown beginner) and partly on the newspaper or magazine. Most newspapers will, if pressed, pay National Union of Journalist rates. How do you know what they are? If you are a freelance member of the NUJ you will be able to get their annual Guide; if not, then simply ask the editor for NUJ rates and trust him to deal honestly with you. The size of payment is likely to depend very much with magazines on the size of circulation, but if it is not made clear, then ask. And you get more if you supply your own photographs to illustrate your piece.

Of course, a one-time use means that there is no question of reversion of rights. Once the piece is published, you are free to offer second serial rights elsewhere. However, rights will revert to you if a magazine has accepted material from you, but has decided later not to publish it. In such a circumstance, you may be offered a 'kill fee' (or compensation for cancellation), and if not, you should ask for one. It will normally be a proportion of what you would have received on publication, and the proportion will vary with the standards of the newspaper or magazine (try for at least 50% of the full fee).

WARNING

Some magazines, when paying for use of an article or story, ask you to sign a note on the back of the cheque. This friendly little paragraph says that you accept the payment and in return grant the magazine the full copyright in your piece. Have nothing to do with this. Simply cross out the note without signing it. The magazine won't stop the payment, nor are they likely for that reason to refuse to publish either your present work or anything that you may submit to them in future. They're simply trying it on.

14   Where to Get Help

Where should you turn for help if you are in any kind of difficulty over the agreement that you have been offered or that you have signed (no matter how long ago you signed it)? Of course, if you have an agent, he should have seen to it that the agreement for your book is a reasonable one, with none of the traps in it against which I have warned, and he should certainly understand everything in it. Moreover, negotiations with publishers and the resolution of disputes between his authors and their publishers are an important part of his job. So if you have any problems you go first to your agent.

But many authors do not have an agent. If you haven't got one, then the first person to whom you should turn for help is your publisher. Remember three very important points in the Publishers Association's Code of Practice: firstly, *book publishing is so varied in its scope that contracts are likely to contain many variations*; secondly, *the publisher should ensure that an author who is not professionally represented has a proper opportunity for explanation of the terms of the contract and the reasons for each provision*; and thirdly, *ideally, terms (for the resolution of disputes) will be agreed privately between the parties*. The first of these quotations is an admission that there is no such thing as a standard form of agreement, the second recognizes that wording which may be crystal clear to the publisher is not necessarily so to the author, and the third suggests that some kind of dialogue will take place if there is disagreement between the parties. What the Code of Practice doesn't mention (and in fairness it could hardly be expected to) is that the terms of an agreement are always open to discussion, and can often be amended before the final signing, though it does include a senten e which allows for amendment at a later date. In some cases the discussion may be fruitless, with the publisher refusing to budge, but you can be pretty sure that he will not cancel the whole deal, unless you are over-persistent, refusing to take no for an answer. And he will not be surprised that you want to get an improvement in your terms – he may not realize that, as I pointed out in the Foreword of this book, most of his authors regard him as the Enemy, but he is aware that the climate has changed in the past few years, and that authors, whom in any case he has always thought of as greedy, are now much less willing than they used to be to accept his terms as though they were carved in stone. So, whatever the problem you have with your contract, go to your publisher, tell him frankly what is bothering you, and with any luck you will be able to come to an amicable solution.

But supposing you have not got an agent and are scared of your publisher? Or what do you do if you have tried to get your publisher to change the contract, which he has refused to do, but you still feel that you have a reasonable point? If you are a member of a writers' circle, you could see if any other member can give you advice; and since many such groups include long-established and successful authors, this is a real possibility. But you may feel that you need a greater degree of expertise. And if you are not so much in the middle of discussions as embroiled in a real dispute, you will certainly need expert help. The publisher may suggest placing the problem first of all before the PA Informal Disputes Settlement Scheme, a body which is not necessarily going to favour the publisher in its decisions – it will try extremely hard to be neutral and fair – but you may nevertheless prefer someone who will be committed from the start to fighting your corner. If you refuse the PA Informal Disputes option, you may next turn to the arbitration clause in your contract – and may immediately find yourself facing a new difficulty, depending on whether your agreement allows for a single nominee or one from each side; in the former case, you might have to accept the publisher's suggested arbitrator, simply because he is likely to know more qualified individuals than you do, while in the latter case it might not be easy to decide whom to nominate.

Or if the case does not seem suitable for arbitration, you may need legal advice. You can go a lawyer (especially if you choose one of those firms which has specialized for years in literary matters, and will therefore be likely to understand your difficulties and know what can be done and what cannot), but this is likely to be a very expensive business.

There is, however, a simpler answer to all these difficult situations, and that is to be a member of the Society of Authors. You can join as soon as you are offered a contract, and before signing it you can send it to the Society and get them to vet it for you. If you have a dispute with your publisher, the Society will advise you, act on your behalf if necessary, help you to find an arbitrator, and even provide you with legal representation if the matter goes to law. However, I should make it clear that the Society will not act in any dispute in which you are involved which is already in progress at the time you join – in other words, you shouldn't join simply because you are in the middle of a major disagreement with your publisher and want the Society to take over the conduct of the affair and of any legal action which might result. Join before then, and you are covered – quite apart from the other benefits that you will get. For details write to: The Membership Secretary, the Society of Authors, 84 Drayton Gardens, London SW10 9SB.

Much the same applies to the Writers' Guild of Great Britain (and their organization is particularly appropriate if you are a film or television writer). Their address is: 430 Edgware Road, London W2 1EH.

A Note on Electronic Editions

Electronic rights are a jungle. CD-Roms, ebooks (which include books published on the Internet), print on demand (POD) books, and other electronic versions have developed so rapidly and so comparatively recently that contracts between their producers and authors have not yet settled down into anything like a consistent form. Some brief guidance can be given here, but the terms offered can vary not only according to which form of electronic publishing is in question, but also between different producers in any one format and it will therefore be wise to seek expert and detailed advice regarding each contract. If you have an agent you should be able to rely on him to find a path through the jungle for you, but if you have no such advice available, do not despair. The Society of Authors has produced a booklet on *Electronic Publishing Contracts*, which is free to members, but if you do not belong to the Society can be purchased at a price of £10.

Many of the clauses in the MTA will still be relevant, including such matters as rights of consultation, copyright and moral rights, permissions, accounts, revisions, etc. But there are some basic rules applying to contracts for electronic rights which should be borne in mind:

1. When signing a conventional agreement for the publication of a hardcover or paperback book, try to retain the electronic rights rather than granting them to the publisher, although it would be reasonable to agree not to sell any such rights without consulting him. If you are forced to allow the publisher control of the electronic rights, ensure, if you possibly can, that the relevant clause

allows for negotiation of the division of income from these rights to be agreed between you and the publisher at the time of sale.

2. Do not give away anything other than the right which you are selling, so if you are signing an agreement for the production of a book on the Internet, for instance, you should not give the Internet publisher the right to bring out the book in a hardcover or paperback edition.

3. You will probably have to give the electronic publisher an exclusive licence for the electronic rights in question, but it should last for a limited period (as little as two years, if possible) rather than for the full term of copyright. Make sure that a termination clause similar to that shown in the MTA is included, although it will be necessary to substitute wording referring to minimal sales, rather than to the work being out of print.

4. Have nothing to do with any publisher who wants you to put money up front. Such a concern is a Vanity house. Any agreement concerning electronic rights should provide for an advance against royalties in the usual way.

5. On CD-Roms and POD books the royalties paid will probably be similar to those you would receive on sales of a hardcover book, as set out in the MTA, although stepped increases in the royalty percentages should probably clock in at earlier points on the rising scale. You should expect considerably higher royalties on works sold as ebooks. When sold directly from the publisher's website your royalty should be at least 35%, and if they are produced by publishers who have already brought out hardcover or paperback editions of the work, then you could look for as much as 90% of the selling price.

6. The most important rule is to seek advice before you sign an agreement for electronic rights or enter a negotiation over terms, and that applies especially to any such rights which have developed since this book was written.

Glossary

*of terms commonly used in publishers' agreements
and within the trade*

AAA   The Association of Authors' Agents (*q.v.*)

Advance   A sum of money paid by the publisher to the author on account of his expected earnings (i.e. royalties and, usually, income from sub-licences) from the book in question.

ALCS   The Authors' Licensing and Collecting Agency (*q.v.*)

Agreement   The document signed by the author and the publisher which sets out the terms and conditions under which a book written by the former will be published by the latter.

Assignment   The arrangement by which one of the parties to an agreement passes to a third party the benefit of that agreement.

Association of Authors' Agents, The   A body to which the majority of well-known literary agents belong. Its objects are to maintain standards of behaviour and to protect its members.

Author's copies   The complimentary copies supplied by the publisher, free of charge and free of royalty, to the author at the time of publication.

Authors' Licensing and Collecting Society, The   The organization which collects and distributes to the authors concerned moneys due to them from Public Lending Rights (and certain other rights) which arise in foreign countries, and authors' share of money collected by the Copyright Licensing Agency (*q.v.*).

180

Blurb   The advertising copy which the publisher uses on the jacket or cover of a book, in his catalogue and in various other ways. A blurb is not to be confused with a synopsis (*q.v.*). It usually consists of some indication of what the book is about, couched in terms (often exaggeratedly enthusiastic) designed to intrigue the potential reader.

Bookclub rights   The right to licence a bookclub to sell a cheap edition of a book. Bookclub rights are usually included in Volume rights (*q.v.*)

Cheap editions   This term is almost always taken to refer to hardcover copies sold at a price below the original published price. It is not normally applied to paperback editions (whether mass market or trade) or to bookclub editions.

CLA   The Copyright Licensing Agency (*q.v.*)

Co-edition   A book produced simultaneously, in order to reduce costs, for two or more publishers and for different areas of the world or languages. A co-edition may be produced by a publisher or by a packager.

Conflicting work   A later book by the author which might be considered to be so similar in content to the book which is the subject of the agreement that it might damage its sales.

Contract   Another word for Agreement (*q.v.*)

Copy-edited   A typescript is described as 'copy-edited' when it has been prepared for the printer by a copy-editor, employed by the publisher to correct such matters as punctuation and spelling, to check facts, to mark special setting instructions, and on occasion to rewrite the work of careless, inaccurate and illiterate authors.

Copyright   The exclusive right owned by an author (or composer, or artist, or other creative individual) to control and benefit from the use, whether directly or by others, of his work.

Copyright Licensing Agency, The   The organization which licenses the otherwise unlawful photocopying of copyright material, passing the resulting income in due shares to the authors and publishers concerned.

Copyright notice   The notice printed in a book (or in

respect of a story or article in a magazine or newspaper) which attributes the ownership of the copyright to the holder thereof.

Delivery date The date specified in the agreement by which the typescript of the work is to be delivered by the author to the publisher.

Determine A term used in some legal documents in place of 'terminate'.

Edition Each edition of a book, when the term is correctly used, differs substantially from the previous edition. *See also* Impression *and* Revised edition.

Export market In British publishers' agreements the Export market (in which Export sales are made) usually refers to any territories outside the United Kingdom of Great Britain and Northern Ireland and the Irish Republic.

Extent The length of a book, usually expressed in so many thousand words in the case of a typescript and in pages in the case of a printed book.

First refusal Another term for Option (*q.v.*).

First serial rights The rights which cover the sale of material to a magazine or newspaper for publication prior to publication in book form. *See also* Serial rights.

Foreign rights Another term for Translation rights (*q.v.*). Not to be confused with the sale of the British publisher's edition of a book in foreign countries, which comes under Export sales.

Format Primarily the shape of a published book, which is determined by the size of the paper used. The term is also often employed in agreements in reference to either hardcover or paperback editions.

Free copies These include copies of a book sent out for review, copies distributed for publicity purposes and the author's complimentary copies.

Grant of rights In an agreement the Grant of rights covers full details of the licence which the author gives the publisher, which specifies the extent of the rights, languages and territories in which the publisher may operate.

Hardback Another term for the more usual Hardcover.

Hardcover The term generally indicates that the book is

bound in boards covered with cloth or imitation cloth, and is equipped with a jacket.

Home market For British publishers the Home market (in which Home sales are made) usually consists of the United Kingdom of Great Britain and Northern Ireland, plus the Irish Republic.

Impression A reprint of a book, without changes to the text, is termed an Impression. Technically, if any alterations are made, the term Edition should be used, but in practice most publishers continue to talk of Impressions if the changes are slight ones.

Jacket The loose paper wrapper which is placed around a hardcover book.

Large-print books The editions of books which are produced, mainly for sale to libraries, with a large size of print which makes them more easily readable by the partially sighted.

Licence period The length of time for which a publisher, or his sub-licensee, may exercise the rights granted under the agreement.

Liquidation When a company collapses, usually into bankruptcy, it goes into liquidation and ceases to trade.

Mass market paperbacks Paperbacks which are printed in very large quantities, using economical materials and methods in order to keep the cost down. *See also* Trade paperbacks.

Minimum Terms Agreement A form of agreement drawn up by the Society of Authors and the Writers' Guild setting out the minimum terms which they feel should be offered by publishers and which should be acceptable to authors. Several publishers have signed MTAs with the Society and the Guild, with minor variations in each case.

Moral rights Moral rights cover both those of 'paternity' (the right of the author to be identified as the creator of the work, whether it is published in full or in part) and those of 'integrity' (the right of the author to be protected against distortion or mutilation of his work in any adaptation or other treatment of it). Authors have to 'assert' their rights of paternity, which they do by requiring the publisher to print a notice to that effect in all copies of their books.

MTA Minimum Terms Agreement (*q.v.*)

NBA   Net Book Agreement (*q.v.*).

Net Book Agreement   The agreement under which publishers and booksellers maintained the set retail prices for books. Initiated in 1900, it was abandoned in 1995, with the result that many books (mostly bestsellers) are now available at heavily discounted prices, primarily in the chain bookshops.

Option   The promise which an author gives a publisher to allow him to have the first opportunity of considering the author's next book for publication.

Outright payment or sale   A one-time payment by a publisher to an author, usually taken to mean that the publisher is buying all rights, including copyright.

Overseas sales   Overseas or export sales are those books sold in the Export market (*q.v.*).

PA   The Publishers Association (*q.v.*).

Packager   An entrepreneur who conceives, commissions and produces books which he then sells to publishers in various countries.

Paperbacks   Books bound in stiff paper (known as a cover, rather than a jacket). Paperbacks may be Mass Market paperbacks (*q.v.*) or Trade paperbacks (*q.v.*).

Permissions   The rights granted to an author or publisher by the copyright holder or his representative to reproduce copyright material.

Piracy   The publication of a book without permission having been given by either the publisher or the author and without the payment of any fees. The pirates are to be found principally in Far Eastern countries.

PLR   Public Lending Right (*q.v.*).

PLS   Publishers Licensing Society (*q.v.*).

Preamble   The first part of an agreement which identifies the parties to it and the subject of the agreement.

Proprietor   In some publishing agreements the author is referred to (especially if he has turned himself into a limited company, or if the agreement is being signed on his behalf by someone else) as 'the Proprietor'. The term will often be used by the publisher to refer to himself when sub-licensing another publisher.

Public Lending Right   The right, enshrined in law, for authors to receive payment out of Government funds for the borrowings of their books from Public Libraries.

Published price The recommended retail price of a book.

Publishers Association, The The fraternal, advisory body to which most of the major publishers (but not all) belong.

Publishers Licensing Society The organization which represents publishers and their interests in the Copyright Licensing Agency and which distributes to its members the moneys due to them which result from the licensing of photocopying.

Remainders The remaining copies of an edition which has either ceased to sell or is selling so slowly as to be uneconomic. The publisher disposes of his overstock at knock-down prices to a remainder merchant, who then releases them to the public at very cheap prices, usually through special bookshops.

Reprographic rights Reprography is principally concerned with photo-copying.

Reserves against returns The withholding of a proportion of royalties until it becomes certain that the books have been sold and will not be returned by the bookseller or wholesaler.

Returns Unsold books sent back to the publisher for credit by booksellers and wholesalers.

Reversion The return of rights to the author following the cancellation of the agreement.

Review copies Copies of a book sent to newspapers, magazines and other interested parties in the hope that they will publish reviews of the book. The term is also used to cover the sample copies sent to potential sub-licensees.

Revised editions Any alteration to a book before it is reprinted makes it technically a revised edition. In practice, however, the term is not usually used unless the alteration is fairly substantial.

Rights Each of the varied uses of a book, or of a part thereof, is covered by a right which may be granted to the publisher (and re-granted, or sub-licensed by him) or retained by the author.

Royalties The sum paid to the author by the publisher for each copy of his book which is sold. The royalty is usually calculated as a percentage either of the published price of the book, or of the price received by the publisher. The system of rewarding authors by the payment of royalties did not become widespread until the end of the 19th century, prior to which publishers either bought the copyright outright or paid the author a lump sum to cover each impression or edition of the book.

Royalty-free copies No royalties are payable on review copies, copies given away for publicity purposes, the author's complimentary copies, copies which are returned by booksellers or wholesalers (except in those cases where the publisher accepts responsibility for returns which come in after the reserve against returns has been fed back into the royalty statements), or copies which are damaged or destroyed.

Second serial rights The rights which cover the sale of material to a magazine or newspaper for publication after publication in book form or prior publication in a magazine or newspaper. However many times the material is re-sold, each sale is still of *second* serial rights (not third, fourth or umpteenth). *See also* Serial rights.

Serial rights Serial rights cover the sale of material, which range from the whole book to a single short extract from it, or any article or short story, to a newspaper or magazine. The word 'serial' does not necessarily imply a series of instalments in succeeding issues of a journal, but can be taken in this context to mean 'newspaper or magazine'.

Setting The process of turning a typescript into printing type is known as setting or composition.

Sheets Before a book has been bound it consists of printed sheets of paper, and may sometimes be sold in that form for binding by the purchaser. Sheets are sometimes sold flat and sometimes 'folded and collated' in which case the sheets have been folded into signatures which have then been grouped together to form the unbound book. Yet another possibility is that these folded and collated sheets will be sewn, thus completing a further stage in the binding process.

Society of Authors, The The senior organization (founded in 1884) for authors working in all genres. A trade union, it is not affiliated to the TUC.

Sub-licences When the publisher of a book sells any of the rights of which the author has granted him the control, these are sub-licences, so called because they derive from the principal licence granted by the author.

Subsidiary rights Some consider that the term 'subsidiary rights' covers all rights granted to a publisher other than the main right to publish his own editions of the work. Others exclude either all or some of paperback, bookclub, US and translation rights from the list of those which they would call 'subsidiary'.

Synopsis A summary of the contents of a book, usually prepared by the author in the hope of persuading a publisher to commission him to write it.

Termination The cancellation of the agreement.

Territories The specified areas of the world in which the publisher is granted the right to sell his editions of the book and to sub-license others to exercise various rights. The territories may be restricted further by a reference to the language in which the rights are granted.

Title Publishers use the word 'title' not only in the sense of the name of the book, but also as a synonym for 'a work in book form'.

Trade paperback A paperback edition usually produced by the publisher of the hardcover edition, frequently in a larger format than a mass market paperback, and priced at a figure somewhere between the retail cost of a hardcover and that of a mass market version. It has largely supplanted the cheap edition which a hardcover publisher would have produced in the days before the advent of the mass market paperback revolutionized the book trade.

Translation rights The rights which cover the sale of the book to a foreign language publisher who will publish it in a version which has been translated into his own language.

United States rights The rights which cover the sale of a book to an American publisher.

Volume rights The term normally covers the right to produce hardcover and paperback editions and to sub-license paperback and bookclub editions, but these sub-licensing rights are not always included. If the licence granted is for World English language rights, the volume rights are sometimes taken to include the right to sub-license an American edition or editions. If the licence granted is for World rights without any restriction on languages, the volume rights are sometimes taken to include the right to sell translation rights.

Warranty The commitment that an author makes and which the original publisher may pass on to any sub-licensees that his material is original, does not infringe anyone else's copyright, and does not include anything harmful or in any way unlawful.

Work In most publishing contracts the book in question is referred to as 'the Work'.

World rights World rights may be expressed as 'all rights throughout the World' in which case there are clearly no restrictions on the publisher who is granted such rights. More often World rights are restricted in some way: for instance, World Volume rights would not necessarily include many of the normal subsidiary rights, while World English language rights would clearly not allow the publisher to sell translation rights.

Writers' Guild of Great Britain, The The junior of the two principal organizations for authors (founded in 1959), with special interest for writers for the large and small screens. A trade union, it is affiliated to the TUC.

Index

(for definitions see Glossary)